Name ____

Riddle: When should a battery call the doctor?

___ ___ ___ ___   ___ ___   ___ ___ ___   ___
72 11 91 52   86 58   11 33 25   33

___ ___ ___   ___ ___ ___ ___ ___ ___
36 33 41   33 58 58 33 10 20

___ ___   ___ ___ ___ ___
44 43   33 10 86 41

___ ___ ___ ___ ___ ___ ___ ___ ___ ___ ___
86 52 41 86 60 91 25 58 86 44 52

A $36 - 3$	B $39 - 3$	C $13 - 3$	D $46 - 5$	E $98 - 7$
F $48 - 5$	G $66 - 6$	H $15 - 4$	I $88 - 2$	K $29 - 9$
N $58 - 6$	O $49 - 5$	S $28 - 3$	T $59 - 1$	W $79 - 7$

Skill: 1 digit from 2 digit, no regrouping

Name ______________________________

Tongue Twister:

s l i m   s a m
81 82 76 99   81 42 99

s h a v e d   s i x
81 21 42 35 66 51   81 76 x

s l i p p e r y   c h i n s
81 82 76 43 43 66 54 59   30 21 76 55 81

i n   s e v e n
76 55   81 66 35 66 55

s e c o n d s.
81 66 30 33 55 51 81.

A 48 − 6 = 42	**C** 35 − 5 = 30	**D** 53 − 2 = 51	**E** 68 − 2 = 66	**H** 29 − 8 = 21
I 79 − 3 = 76	**L** 85 − 3 = 82	**M** 99 − 0 = 99	**N** 58 − 3 = 55	**O** 39 − 6 = 33
P 48 − 5 = 43	**R** 57 − 3 = 54	**S** 89 − 8 = 81	**V** 36 − 1 = 35	**Y** 59 − 0 = 59

Name ____

A Happy Thought:

44 80 26 73

50 42 42 58 65 77 14 52 33 73 42

50 80 73 52 21 33 73 65 77 14 –

58 65 52 36 42 77 36 80 33

50 73 65 42 77 13 .

A 56 − 23	**D** 28 − 15	**E** 96 − 54	**F** 87 − 37	**G** 75 − 61
H 92 − 71	**I** 75 − 10	**L** 69 − 11	**N** 89 − 12	**O** 99 − 19
R 87 − 14	**S** 89 − 37	**T** 98 − 62	**U** 38 − 12	**Y** 98 − 54

Skill: 2 digit from 2 digit, no regrouping

Name ______________________________

A Daffynition:

R	E	I	N	D	E	E	r	–	A		C	O	L	D
3	34	19	82	10	34	34	3		44		23	15	57	10

H	O	r	S	E		W	E	A	r	I	N	G		A
63	15	3	25	34		2	34	44	3	19	82	30		44

T	E	L	E	V	I	S	I	O	N
0	34	57	34	58	19	25	19	15	82

A	N	T	E	N	N	A
44	82	0	34	82	82	44

A $76 - 32$ = 44	**C** $84 - 61$ = 23	**D** $97 - 87$ = 10	**E** $55 - 21$ = 34	**G** $72 - 42$ = 30
H $88 - 25$ = 63	**I** $79 - 60$ = 19	**L** $89 - 32$ = 57	**N** $98 - 16$ = 82	**O** $25 - 10$ = 15
R $75 - 72$ = 03	**S** $65 - 40$ = 25	**T** $15 - 15$ = 0	**V** $99 - 41$ = 58	**W** $83 - 81$ = 2

Name ____________________

Skill: 1 digit and 2 digit addends, regrouping

A Happy Thought:

Y O U   H A V E   A
100 53 84   82 40 25 31   40

S P E C I A L   S O N G
74 30 31 60 70 40 72   74 53 27 62

T O   S I N G – S I N G
55 53   74 70 27 62 – 74 70 27 62

O U T !
53 84 55

A 31 + 9 40	C 56 + 4 60	E 25 + 6 31	G 53 + 9 62	H 74 + 8 82
I 62 + 8 70	L 66 + 6 72	N 19 + 8 27	O 46 + 7 53	P 23 + 7 30
S 65 + 9 74	T 48 + 7 55	U 79 + 5 84	V 16 + 9 25	Y 97 + 3 100

Name ______________________________

Skill: 2 digit addends, regrouping

A Tongue Twister:

munch
munch
Not bad.

B	e	A	s	t	l	e	S
46	102	53	74	80	83	102	74

B	l	t	e		b	u	n	c	h	e	s
46	83	80	102		46	95	50	55	90	102	74

o	f		b	A	K	e	d
34	61		46	53	65	102	41

b	u	t	t	e	r	e	d
46	95	80	80	102	70	102	41

b	A	n	A	n	A	S
46	53	50	53	50	53	74.

A: 17 + 36 = 53	B: 29 + 17 = 46	C: 27 + 28 = 55	D: 22 + 19 = 41	E: 63 + 39 = 102
F: 34 + 27 = 61	H: 32 + 58 = 90	I: 55 + 28 = 83	K: 29 + 36 = 65	N: 25 + 25 = 50
O: 15 + 19 = 34	R: 27 + 43 = 70	S: 48 + 26 = 74	T: 26 + 54 = 80	U: 66 + 29 = 95

Name ______________________________

Skill: 2 digit addends, regrouping

Riddle: What did Ben Franklin say when he discovered electricity?

b	e	N		W	A	S		t	o	O
53	71	61		57	84	67		50	42	42

S	H	O	c	K	e	d		t	O
67	86	42	74	30	71	98		50	42

S	A	Y		A	N	Y	t	H	I	N	g
67	84	55		84	61	55	50	86	72	61	43.

A 58 + 26 = 84	**B** 24 + 29 = 53	**C** 45 + 29 = 74	**D** 79 + 19 = 98	**E** 23 + 48 = 71
G 15 + 28 = 43	**H** 67 + 19 = 86	**I** 33 + 39 = 72	**K** 15 + 15 = 30	**N** 22 + 39 = 61
O 27 + 15 = 42	**S** 38 + 29 = 67	**T** 25 + 25 = 50	**W** 18 + 39 = 57	**Y** 39 + 16 = 55

Name ______________________________

Skill: 2 digit addends, regrouping

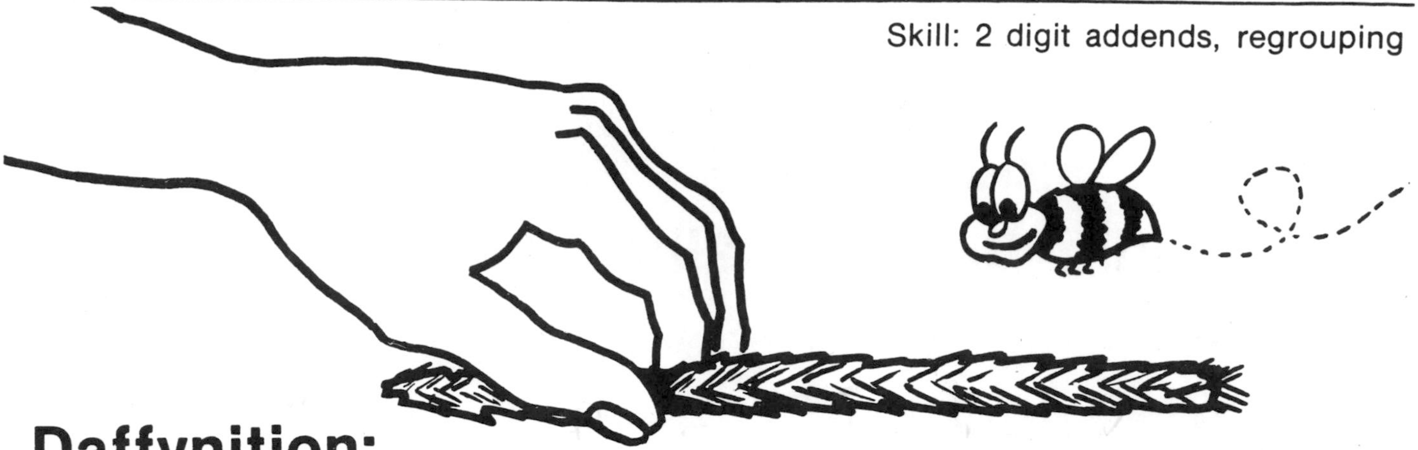

Daffynition:

___ ___ ___ ___ ___ ___ ___ ___ ___ ___ ___ – ___
77 52 77 85 96 134 85 60 91 85 40 – 60

___ ___ ___ ___ ___ ___ ___ ___ ___
31 63 63 31 82 77 52 96 45

___ ___ ___ ___ ___ ___ ___ ___
62 85 60 40 52 91 73 60

___ ___ ___ ___ ___ ___ ___.
90 62 85 60 31 85 40

A 24 + 36	C 37 + 59	E 57 + 28	G 54 + 19	H 49 + 33
I 36 + 16	K 28 + 17	L 75 + 59	N 52 + 39	O 38 + 25
P 18 + 59	R 28 + 12	S 73 + 17	T 15 + 16	W 43 + 19

Name ________________________________

Skill: 2 digit addends, regrouping

Riddle: Why do elephants float on their backs?

T	o		k	e	e	p		t	h	e	i	r
47	100		58	54	54	68		47	75	54	32	30

s	u	n	g	l	a		s	s	e	s
72	46	66	110	81			72	72	54	72

d	r	y	.
31	30	93	

D: 17 + 14 = 31	E: 39 + 15 = 54	G: 55 + 55 = 110	H: 36 + 39 = 75	I: 16 + 16 = 32
K: 29 + 29 = 58	L: 22 + 59 = 81	N: 37 + 29 = 66	O: 56 + 44 = 100	P: 49 + 19 = 68
R: 15 + 15 = 30	S: 23 + 49 = 72	T: 29 + 18 = 47	U: 18 + 28 = 46	Y: 79 + 14 = 93

Name ______________________________

Skill: 3 digit addends, no regrouping

Tongue Twister:

s	e	v	e	n		s	i	l	v	e	r
698	587	339	587	739		698	949	483	339	587	509

s	n	a	k	e	s
698	739	357	799	587	698

s	l	i	o	h	e	r	e	d
698	483	949	228	448	587	509	587	444

s	l	o	w	l	y
698	483	299	593	483	

s	o	u	T	H	w	a	r	d
698	299	559	228	448	593	357	509	444

.

A 234 + 123 = 357	**D** 221 + 223 = 444	**E** 233 + 354 = 587	**H** 320 + 128 = 448	**I** 713 + 236 = 949
K 308 + 491 = 799	**L** 300 + 183 = 483	**N** 524 + 215 = 739	**O** 128 + 171 = 299	**R** 406 + 103 = 509
S 495 + 203 = 698	**T** 125 + 103 = 228	**U** 328 + 231 = 559	**V** 216 + 123 = 339	**W** 272 + 321 = 593

Name ______________________________

Skill: 3 digit addends, no regrouping

Maybe I should get a cart.

Daffynition:

s	h	o	p	p	e	r	–	A
235	281	348	582	582	939	552		253

p	e	r	s	o	n		w	h	o
582	939	552	235	348	574		698	281	348

i	s		g	o	i	n	g		t	o
757	235		356	348	757	574	356		695	348

g	o		b	u	y	–	b	u	y	.
356	348		467	279	266		467	279	266	

A	B	E	G	H
142 + 111 = 253	362 + 105 = 467	125 + 814 = 939	121 + 235 = 356	150 + 131 = 281
I	**N**	**O**	**P**	**R**
421 + 336 = 757	421 + 153 = 574	236 + 112 = 348	450 + 132 = 582	121 + 431 = 552
S	**T**	**U**	**W**	**Y**
135 + 100 = 235	352 + 343 = 695	146 + 133 = 279	153 + 545 = 698	133 + 133 = 266

Skill: 3 digit from 3 digit, no regrouping

Name ____________________

A Tongue Twister:

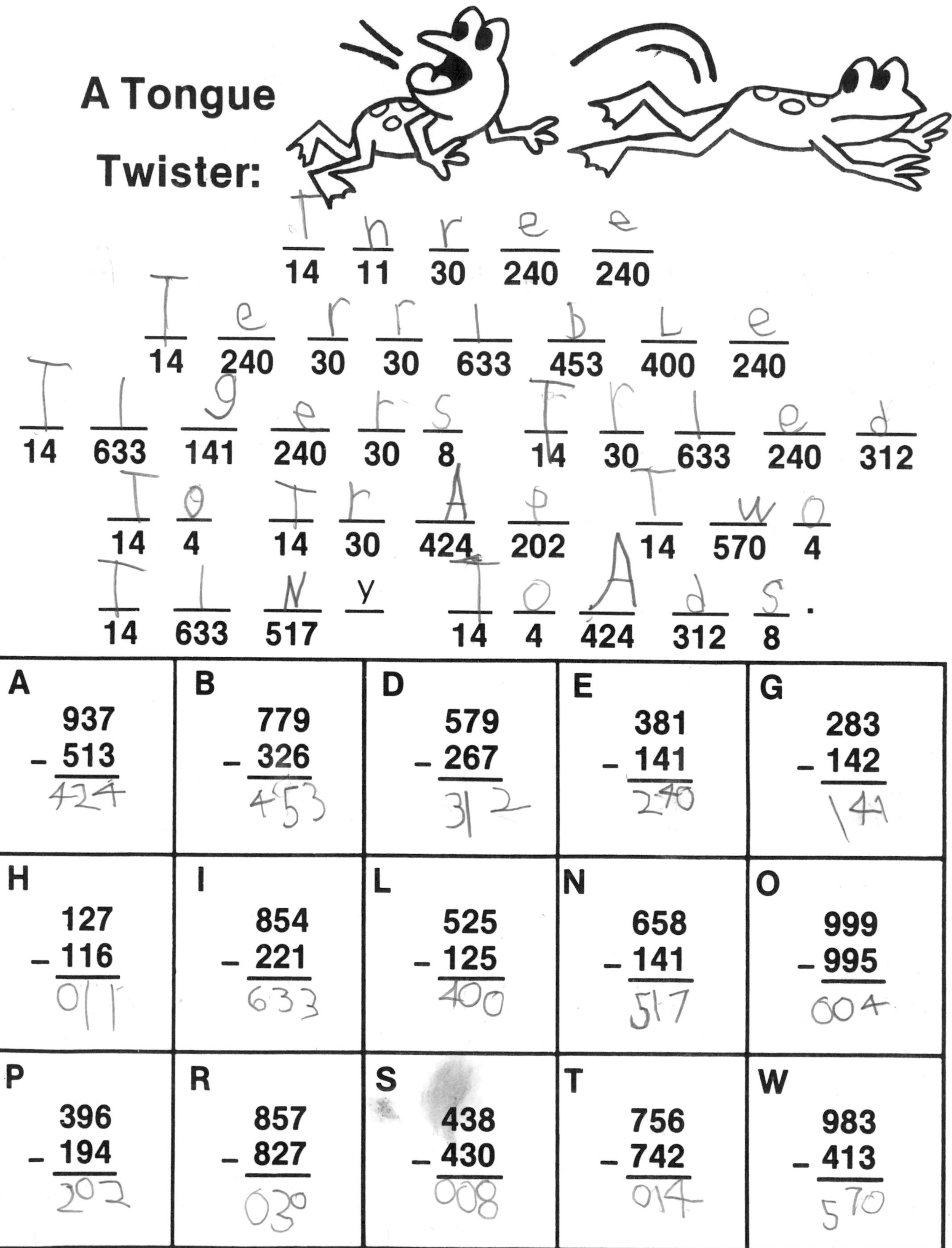

___ ___ ___ ___ ___
14 11 30 240 240

___ ___ ___ ___ ___ ___ ___ ___
14 240 30 30 633 453 400 240

___ ___ ___ ___ ___ ___ ___ ___ ___ ___ ___
14 633 141 240 30 8 14 30 633 240 312

___ ___ ___ ___ ___ ___ ___ ___ ___
14 4 14 30 424 202 14 570 4

___ ___ ___ ___ ___ ___ ___ ___ ___ .
14 633 517 y 14 4 424 312 8

A 937 – 513	B 779 – 326	D 579 – 267	E 381 – 141	G 283 – 142
H 127 – 116	I 854 – 221	L 525 – 125	N 658 – 141	O 999 – 995
P 396 – 194	R 857 – 827	S 438 – 430	T 756 – 742	W 983 – 413

Skill: 3 digit from 3 digit, no regrouping

Name ____

Happy Thought:

___ ___ u ___ ___ ___ ___ ___ ___ ___ ___

244 630   541 23 23 200   1 630 10 303

___ ___ ___ ___   ___ ___ ___

713 820 12 541   820 541 200

___ u ___ ___ ___ ___ ___ ___   ___ ___

474   541 474 303 12 541 23   10 630

___ ___ ___ ___   ___

736 820 340 23   820

___ ___ ___ ___ ___ ___ ___ .

713 820 12 541 1 630 55

A 945 − 125 = 820	**B** 632 − 631 = 003	**D** 358 − 158 = 200	**E** 123 − 100 = 023	**H** 444 − 141 = 303
I 563 − 551 = 012	**K** 743 − 403 = 340	**M** 847 − 111 = 736	**N** 752 − 211 = 541	**O** 951 − 321 = 630
R 883 − 170 = 713	**S** 699 − 225 = 474	**T** 495 − 485 = 010	**W** 176 − 121 = 055	**Y** 367 − 123 = 244

Skill: 3 digit from 3 digit, no regrouping

Name ____________________

Riddle: Why was the strawberry frightened?

___ ___ ___ ___ ___ ___ ___
454 64 600 400 10 113 64

___ ___ ___   ___ ___ ___ ___ ___ ___
555 320 113   782 312 134 555 64 617

___ ___ ___   ___ ___ ___ ___ ___ ___
400   232   350 400 134 555 64 617

___ ___ ___   ___ ___   ___ ___ ___   ___ ___ ___
400 617 64   320   134 555 64   504 400 782

A	B	C	D	E
542 − 142	765 − 311	941 − 341	362 − 130	599 − 535
F	**H**	**I**	**J**	**M**
753 − 403	856 − 301	777 − 457	957 − 453	892 − 110
O	**R**	**S**	**T**	**U**
463 − 151	957 − 340	213 − 100	895 − 761	459 − 449

Name ______________________________

Skill: 2 and 3 addends, regrouping

Riddle: The answer is a walkie-talkie.

But I don't think it's possible.

___ ___ ___ ___   ___ ___   ___ ___ u
491 455 534 850   163 954   886 954

___ ___ ___   ___ ___ ___ ___   ___ ___ u
660 730 850   491 455 730 571   886 954

___ ___ ___ ___ ___   ___
943 838 954 980 980   534

___ ___ ___ ___ ___ ___ ___ ___ ___
943 730 571 850 973 397 730 163 730

___ ___ ___ ___   ___   ___ ___ ___ ___ ___ ?
491 973 850 455   534   838 534 163 973 954

A 418 + 116	C 724 + 219	D 128 + 35	E 414 + 316	G 25 + 635
H 39 + 416	I 349 + 624	N 524 + 47	O 427 + 527	P 289 + 108
R 519 + 319	S 127 + 853	T 811 + 39	W 28 + 463	Y 327 + 559

Name ______________________________

Skill: 2 and 3 digit addends, regrouping to 10's

A Happy Thought:

Are you out there?

858 576 973 973 442   634 442   150 973 973

634 858 576   662 790 371 576 357 83 732

371 ' 638 576   972 576 634   634 442

64 576 576 634 !

A 113 + 37 150	D 46 + 37 83	E 529 + 47 576	F 18 + 644 662	H 29 + 829 858
I 126 + 245 371	L 427 + 546 973	M 29 + 35 64	N 109 + 248 357	O 228 + 214 442
R 447 + 343 790	S 416 + 316 732	T 419 + 215 634	V 219 + 419 638	Y 143 + 829 972

Name ______________________

Skill: 3 digit addends, regrouping to 10's

Happy Thought:

___ ___ ___ ' ___ ___   ___ ___
643 440 588 554 560   781 643

___ ___ ___ ___   ___ ___ ___ ___ ___ ___ ,
242 560 485 324   953 554 278 560 670 250

___ ___ ___ ___ ___   ___ ___ ___ !
485 588 591 560 554   795 278 250

B 123 + 119	D 143 + 107	E 422 + 138	F 839 + 114	I 159 + 119
K 456 + 339	M 362 + 419	N 456 + 214	O 315 + 125	P 282 + 309
R 216 + 338	S 108 + 377	T 107 + 217	U 469 + 119	Y 426 + 217

Name ______________________________

Skill: 3 digit addends, regrouping to 10's

Although marmalade is good too.

Riddle:

W ___ ___ ___   ___ ___   ___ ___ ___ ___ ___
433 788 235   686 361   482 433 535 535 420

___ ___ ___ ___ ___ ___   ___ ___
482 420 853 535 788 686   361 380

___ ___ ___ ___ ___   ___ ___ ___ ___ ___?
235 433 535 894 853   235 361 788 482 235

___ ___ ___ ___   ___ ___ ___.
923 788 483 451   490 788 483

A 369 + 419	B 142 + 309	D 268 + 418	E 429 + 106	H 109 + 324
I 287 + 607	J 321 + 169	L 609 + 314	M 158 + 325	N 264 + 116
O 236 + 125	P 305 + 115	R 409 + 444	S 223 + 259	T 129 + 106

Name ______________________________

Skill: 3 digit addends, regrouping to 10's

What's
all that?

A Tongue Twister:

652   890 666 593 785 950 793   890 394 212 371

890 666 991 874 793 991 442 652 212 666 212 442

890 394 371 910   890 593 394 394 593 991 874 442

991 668   890 666 991 910 874

890 212 890 890 394 371 442 .

A 436 + 216	B 771 + 119	E 157 + 214	F 529 + 139	G 358 + 427
H 845 + 105	I 164 + 429	L 207 + 187	N 525 + 349	O 185 + 806
R 538 + 128	S 223 + 219	T 558 + 235	U 109 + 103	W 705 + 205

Name ______________________________

Skill: 2 and 3 digit addends, regrouping to 100's

Riddle: What did the highway say to the street?

I can't hear anything!

"

___ 600   ___ 509 ___ 317 ___ 269 ___ 984   ___ 623 ___ 509 ___ 317 ___ 623

___ 623 ___ 600 ___ 916 ___ 984 ___ 635 ,

___ 916 ___ 709 ___ 438 ___ 635 ___ 506 ___ 257 ___ 438

___ 429 ___ 984 ___ 984 ___ 236 ___ 600 ___ 438 ___ 935 ."

A	D	E	F	G
153 + 164	462 + 173	591 + 393	274 + 155	743 + 192
H	**I**	**L**	**N**	**O**
251 + 258	390 + 210	193 + 43	258 + 180	235 + 271
R	**T**	**U**	**V**	**W**
334 + 582	362 + 261	80 + 629	176 + 93	163 + 94

Name ______________________________

Skill: 2 and 3 digit addends, regrouping to 100's

Tongue Twister:

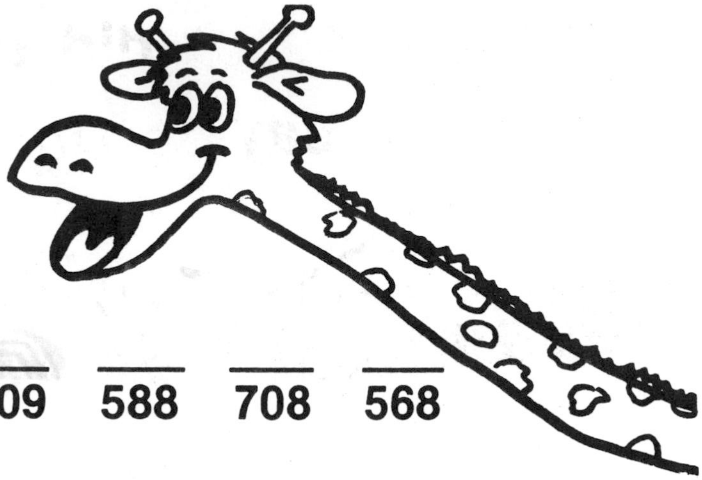

___ ___ ___ ___ ___ ___ ___ ___
924 647 450 406 609 588 708 568

___ ___ ___ ___ ___ ___ ___ ___
924 616 647 450 588 588 609 938

___ ___ ___ ___ ___   ___ ___
924 647 450 306 609   576 227

___ ___ ___ ___ ___ ___ ___ ___
924 616 924 450 227 840 616 406

___ ___ ___ ___ ___ ___ .
924 647 450 829 609 938

A 260 + 190	C 150 + 256	E 532 + 77	F 397 + 191	G 462 + 462
I 240 + 376	L 287 + 281	N 173 + 54	O 386 + 190	P 648 + 181
R 573 + 74	S 767 + 171	T 450 + 390	U 346 + 362	Z 113 + 193

Name ____

Skill: 3 digit addends, regrouping to 100's

A Happy Thought:

___ ___ ___   b   ___ ___ ___   ___ ___ ___ ___
222 409 627   627 609 222   258 377 524 222

___ ___   ___ ___ ___   ___ ___   ___ ___ ___
329 767   436 329 648   500 609   217 409 329

___ ___ ___   ___ ___ ___
436 329 648   377 524 627

___ ___ ___ ___ ___ ___ .
500 849 609 500 938 627

A 283 + 94	D 777 + 161	E 296 + 331	F 483 + 284	H 156 + 253
I 170 + 330	N 279 + 570	O 246 + 83	P 165 + 93	R 372 + 152
S 492 + 117	T 161 + 61	U 394 + 254	W 141 + 76	Y 385 + 51

Name ______________________________

Skill: 3 digit addends, regrouping to 100's

Riddle: Why do monsters forget?

___ ___ ___ ___ ___ ___ ___ ___ ___ ___
929 612 929 944 534 627 605 988 934 867

___ ___ ___ ___   ___ ___   ___ ___ ___
867 504 929 643   988 934   504 934 929

___ ___ ___   ___ ___ ___
929 807 944   807 934 339

___ ___ ___   ___ ___ ___
504 510 627   627 605 929

___ ___ ___ ___ ___   ___ ___ ___ .
504 627 605 929 944   643 988 745

A 343 + 464	D 166 + 173	E 299 + 630	G 585 + 282	H 451 + 154
I 293 + 695	N 583 + 351	O 292 + 212	R 793 + 151	S 350 + 293
T 493 + 134	U 130 + 380	V 351 + 261	X 453 + 292	Y 343 + 191

Name ____

Skill: 3 digit addends, regrouping to 10's and 100's

A Happy Thought:

___ ___ ___ j ___ ___ ___ ___ ___ ___
627 730 697   697 870 641   913 730 304

___ ___ ___ “___ ___ ___ ___ ___
641 405 531   870 697 653 531 711

___ ___ ___” ___ ___ ___ ___ ___.
500 820 706   427 913 427 711 706

A	D	E	H	I
199 + 228	459 + 247	387 + 144	228 + 177	443 + 377
K	**N**	**O**	**P**	**R**
394 + 106	189 + 115	543 + 187	469 + 184	243 + 468
S	**T**	**U**	**W**	**Y**
285 + 585	342 + 299	346 + 351	534 + 379	399 + 228

Name ______________________________

How are "2 plus 2 equal 5" and your left hand alike?
2 + 2 = 5
abcdefghi
Neither is right!

Find the sums.

286 + 302 = 588			6235 + 2644 = 8879
623 + 748 = 1371	584 + 309 = 893	7489 + 6306 = 13795	4928 + 7058 = 11986
782 + 857	350 + 695	7085 + 7164	2343 + 6785
275 + 859	845 + 296	9428 + 9195	2683 + 7970
394 + 785	402 + 698	2975 + 7186	9462 + 3389

Name ____________________

Find the sums.

6
4
9
2
8
3
7
\+ 1

8
3
2
7
5
\+ 6

2
5
8
9
3
\+ 5

6
3
9
4
2
\+ 8

37
48
93
\+ 66

852
694
481
\+ 738

37
86
92
\+ 23

3
5
9
1
2
6
\+7

43
28
\+ 56

54
96
\+ 35

8
4
2
7
6
3
\+9

Skill: 2 digit from 2 digit, regrouping

Name ______________________________

A Tongue Twister:

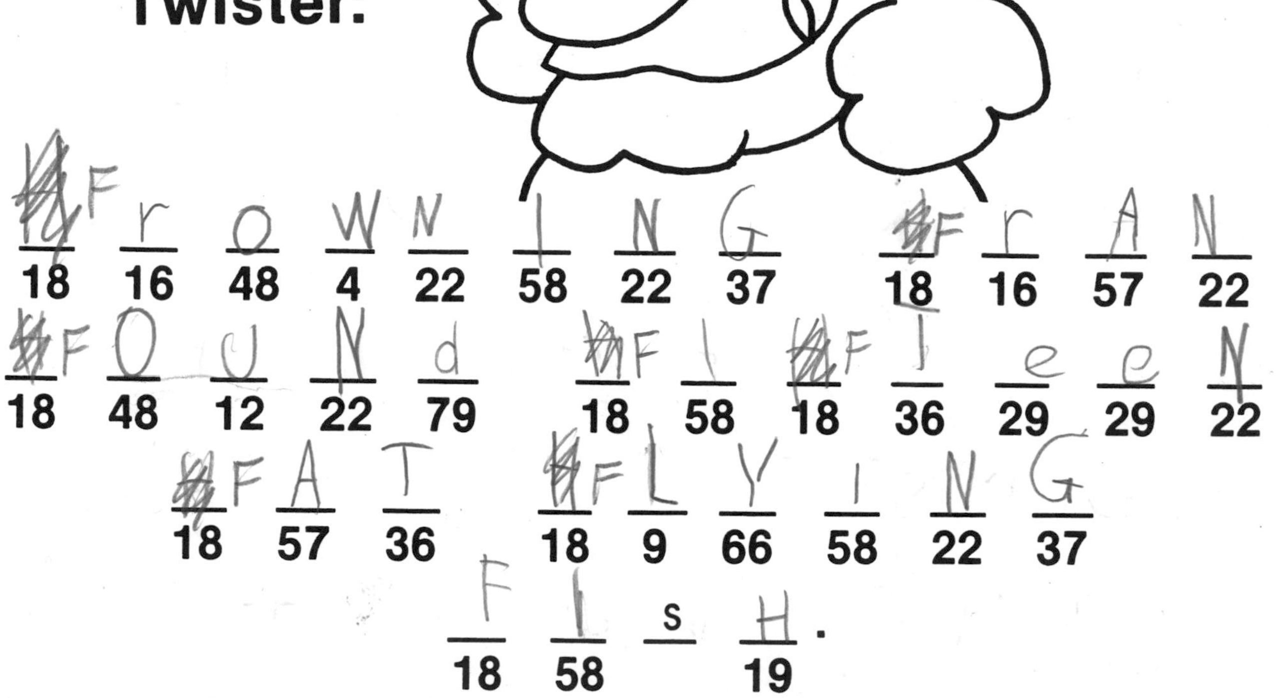

___ ___ ___ ___ ___ ___ ___ ___   ___ ___ ___ ___
18 16 48 4 22 58 22 37   18 16 57 22

___ ___ ___ ___ ___   ___ ___   ___ ___ ___ ___ ___
18 48 12 22 79   18 58   18 36 29 29 22

___ ___ ___   ___ ___ ___ ___ ___ ___
18 57 36   18 9 66 58 22 37

___ ___ S ___ .
18 58   19

A 86 − 29	D 98 − 19	E 47 − 18	F 46 − 28	G 55 − 18
H 88 − 69	I 94 − 36	L 37 − 28	N 60 − 38	O 85 − 37
R 65 − 49	T 84 − 48	U 61 − 49	W 53 − 49	Y 92 − 26

Name ______________________________

RATTLE
RATTLE

A Daffynition:

s	k	e	l	e	t	o	n	–	a
28	56	19	29	19	59	48	9		37

p	e	r	s	o	n		w	h	o		i	s
78	19	17	28	48	9		45	26	48		15	28

i	n	s	i	d	e		o	u	t
15	9	28	15	6	19		48	7	59

A 53 − 16 = 37	**D** 75 − 69 = 6	**E** 88 − 69 = 19	**H** 54 − 28 = 26	**I** 42 − 27 = 15
K 75 − 19 = 56	**L** 44 − 15 = 29	**N** 55 − 46 = 09	**O** 76 − 28 = 48	**P** 96 − 18 = 78
R 94 − 77 = 17	**S** 46 − 18 = 28	**T** 97 − 38 = 59	**U** 26 − 19 = 07	**W** 84 − 39 = 45

Name ______________________________

A Riddle:

W	h	a	t		i	s		B	l	a	c	k
38	25	52	14		8	9		27	56	52	4	29

a	n	d		w	h	i	t	e		a	n	d
52	62	36		38	25	8	14	43		52	62	36

l	i	v	e	s		i	n		t	h	e
56	8	77	43	9		8	62		14	25	43

d	e	s	e	r	t	?
36	43	9	43	6	14	

A lost penguin.

A 81 − 29 = 52	**B** 46 − 19 = 27	**C** 53 − 49 = 04	**D** 65 − 29 = 36	**E** 82 − 39 = 43
H 44 − 19 = 25	**I** 97 − 89 = 8	**K** 45 − 16 = 29	**L** 85 − 29 = 56	**N** 81 − 19 = 62
R 25 − 19 = 06	**S** 77 − 68 = 9	**T** 53 − 39 = 14	**V** 95 − 18 = 77	**W** 86 − 48 = 38

Name ____

A Daffynition:

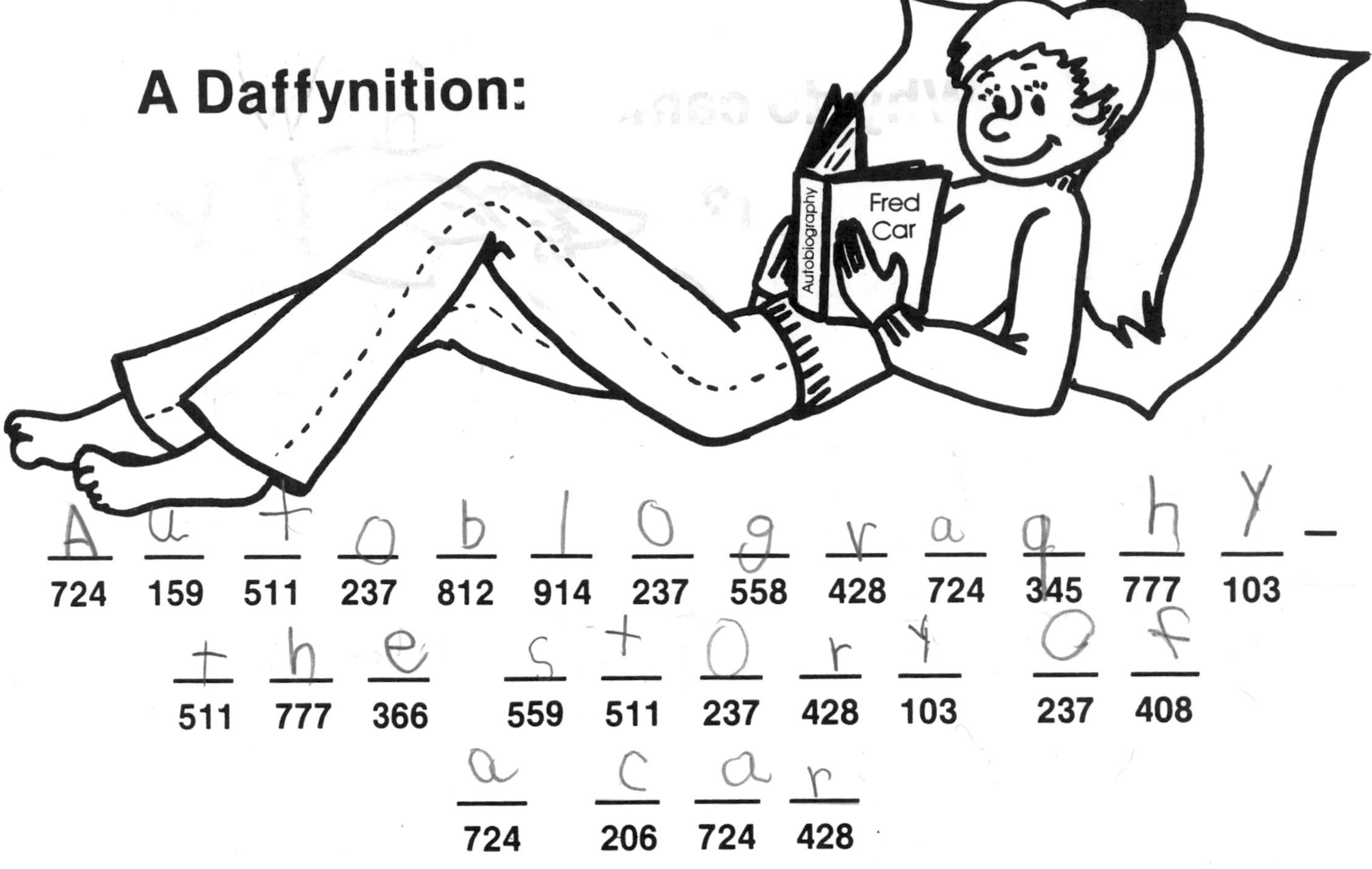

___ ___ ___ ___ ___ ___ ___ ___ ___ ___ ___ ___ ___ –
724 159 511 237 812 914 237 558 428 724 345 777 103

___ ___ ___   ___ ___ ___ ___ ___   ___ ___
511 777 366   559 511 237 428 103   237 408

___   ___ ___ ___
724   206 724 428

A 753 − 29	B 851 − 39	C 252 − 46	E 395 − 29	F 427 − 19
G 584 − 26	H 793 − 16	I 940 − 26	O 274 − 37	P 360 − 15
R 455 − 27	S 598 − 39	T 530 − 19	U 186 − 27	Y 190 − 87

Name ______________________________

Riddle: Why do camels drink water?

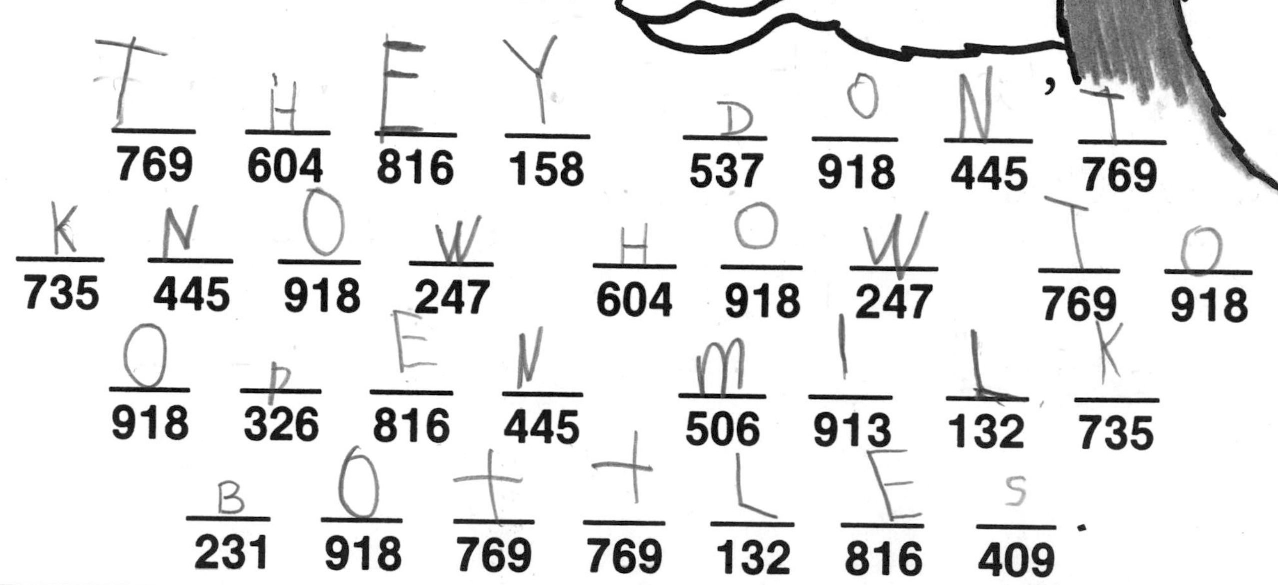

___ ___ ___ ___ ___ ___ ___ ' ___
769 604 816 158 537 918 445 769

___ ___ ___ ___ ___ ___ ___ ___ ___
735 445 918 247 604 918 247 769 918

___ ___ ___ ___ ___ ___ ___ ___
918 326 816 445 506 913 132 735

___ ___ ___ ___ ___ ___ ___ .
231 918 769 769 132 816 409

B 250 − 19	D 555 − 18	E 864 − 48	H 633 − 29	I 941 − 28
K 764 − 29	L 181 − 49	M 525 − 19	N 473 − 28	O 936 − 18
P 352 − 26	S 444 − 35	T 796 − 27	W 282 − 35	Y 193 − 35

Skill: 2 digit from 3 digit, regrouping

Name ____

Riddle:

___ ___ ___ ___   ___ ___   ___
157 119 544 405   548 233   544

___ ___ ___ ___ ___ ___   ___ ___ ___
233 718 544 446 316 909   233 316 544

___ ___ ___ ___ ___ ___ ___
931 ___ 936 233 405 316 446

___ ___ ___ ___ ___ ___ ?
718 544 228 228 316 909

___   ___ ___ ___ ___ ___ ___ ___   ___ ___
544   718 119 548 718 349 316 936   ___ 657

___ ___ ___   ___ ___ ___
405 119 316   233 316 544

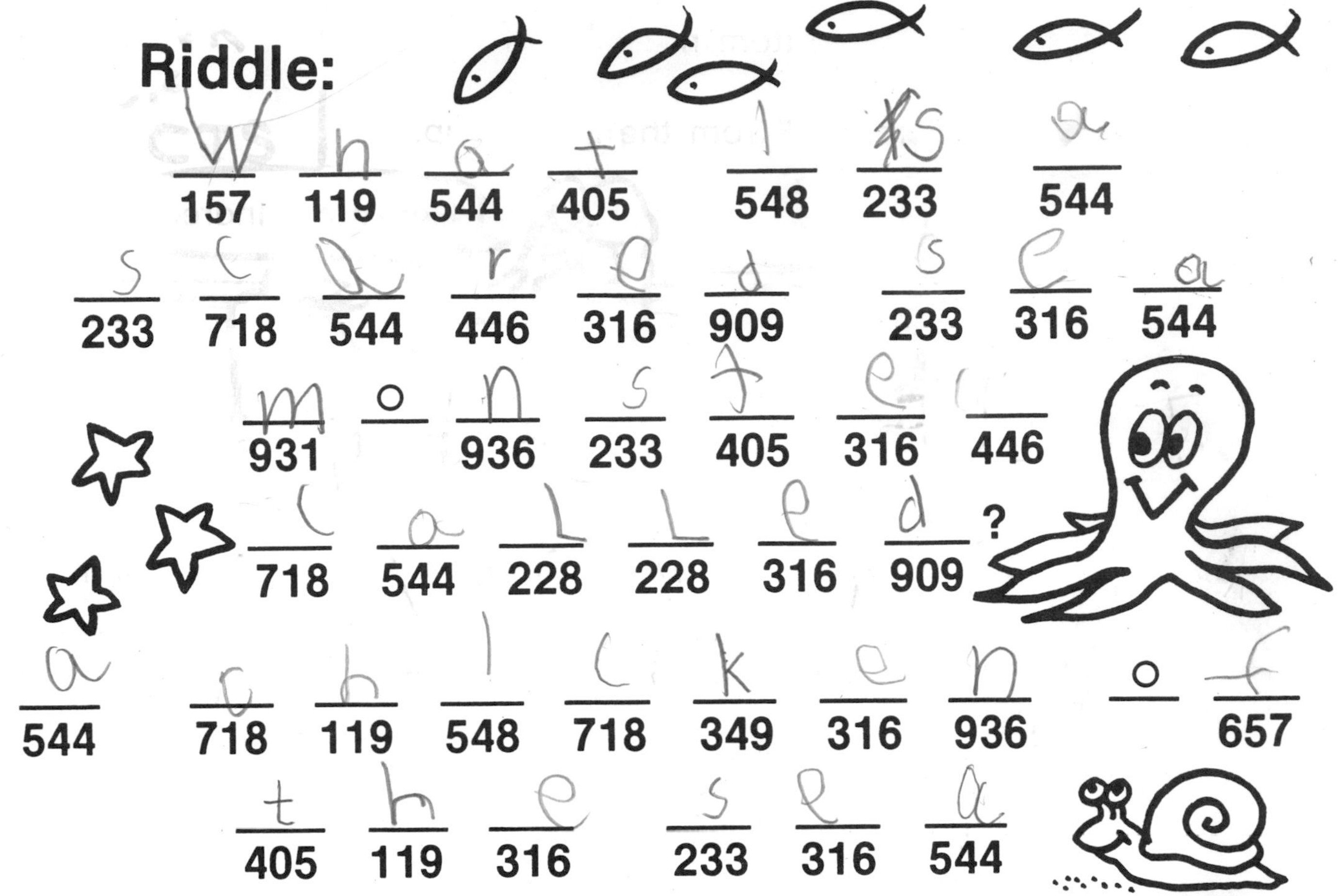

A 563 − 19	**C** 735 − 17	**D** 927 − 18	**E** 341 − 25	**F** 683 − 26
H 136 − 17	**I** 586 − 38	**K** 375 − 26	**L** 256 − 28	**M** 950 − 19
N 961 − 25	**R** 493 − 47	**S** 292 − 59	**T** 444 − 39	**W** 194 − 37

Name ______________________________

THESE ARE THE FACTS:

- In subtraction, when the bottom number is bigger, you have to borrow!
- To check your answers, add from the bottom up.

BANK OF FACTS
Here's a ten!
Here's a hundred!

624 − 237	624 − 237 = 7	624 − 237 = 387

384 − 126	593 − 87	826 − 197	428 − 61	709 − 454
907 − 688	623 − 358	290 − 128	830 − 96	524 − 375
411 − 260	473 − 96	650 − 567	301 − 126	948 − 579
803 − 98	526 − 368	700 − 243	900 − 161	600 − 374

How can you tell if it's right?
To double-check, **add** from the bottom **up**!
3064
-2347
717
+

8795
− 3452

9688
− 2057

7640
− 2605
5035

6839
− 2479
4360

8230
− 7519
0711

5761
− 4299

8596
− 2348

It pays to proofread problems! Perfect your Practice!

6057
− 1808

3085
− 1507

4306
− 1552

9205
− 4621

8621
− 5934

7413
− 3895

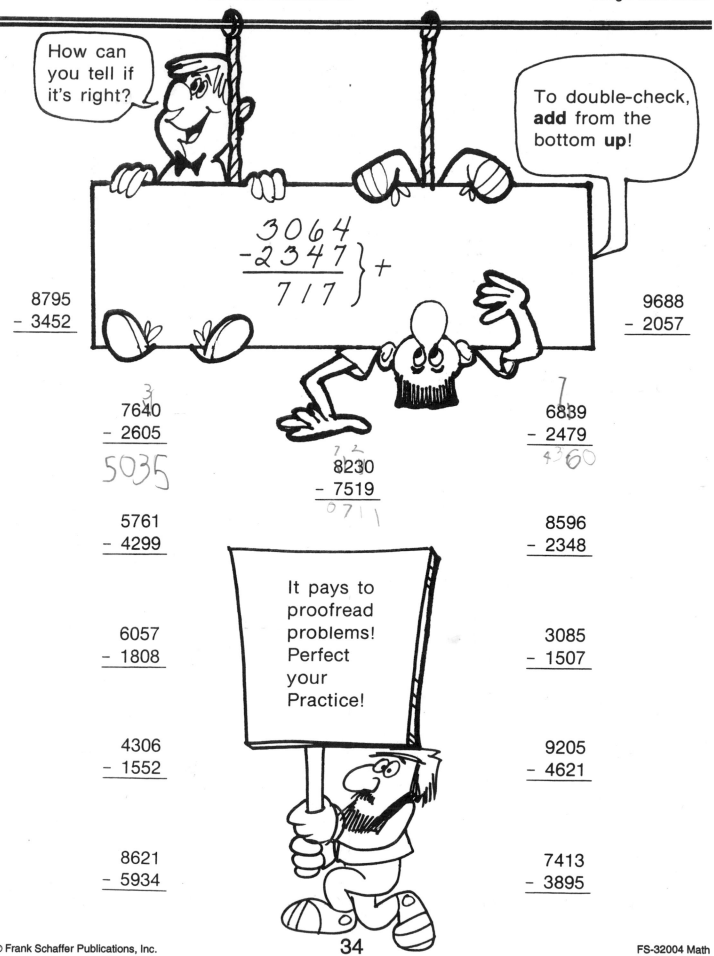

Name ______________________ Skill: Multiplying by 0, 1 and 2

Hop to It!

Write each product.

A.
0 x 0 = 0
8 x 0 = 0
2 x 0 = 0
7 x 0 = 0
4 x 0 = 0
5 x 0 = 0
9 x 0 = 0
1 x 0 = 0
6 x 0 = 0
3 x 0 = 0

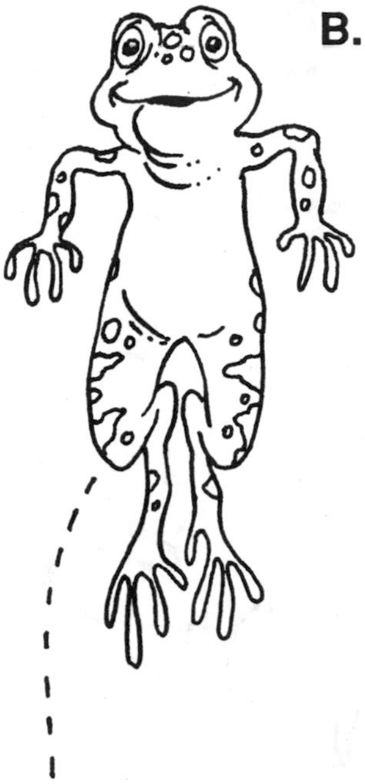

B.
7 x 1 = 7
1 x 1 = 1
5 x 1 = 5
6 x 1 = 6
3 x 1 = 3
8 x 1 = 8
0 x 1 = 0
4 x 1 = 4
2 x 1 = 2
9 x 1 = 9

C.
4 x 2 = 8 (4+4 = 8)
9 x 2 = 18
3 x 2 = 6
0 x 2 = 0
8 x 2 = 16
2 x 2 = 4
6 x 2 = 12
1 x 2 = 2
5 x 2 = 10
7 x 2 = 14

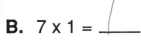

Solve each problem.

D. 1 x 5 = 5	**E.** 2 x 1 = 2	**F.** 0 x 9 = 0	**G.** 2 x 4 = 8	**H.** 1 x 7 = 7	**I.** 2 x 8 = 16
J. 2 x 2 = 4	**K.** 1 x 0 = 0	**L.** 2 x 5 = 10	**M.** 1 x 3 = 3	**N.** 2 x 9 = 18	**O.** 1 x 2 = 2
P. 2 x 3 = 6	**Q.** 0 x 8 = 0	**R.** 2 x 7 = 14	**S.** 2 x 6 = 16		Score 46/46

Brainwork! If a number is multiplied by 2, the answer will always end in one of five numbers. Write the five numbers. 0, 2, 4, 6, 8

Name ______________________________

A Riddle

What has thirty-six legs and goes to picnics?

What could it be?

___   ___ ___ ___ ___ ___ ___   ___ ___ ___   ___ ___ ___ ___ ___ ___

6   8 12 18 2 10 16   6 18 14   3 6 5 7 9 16

A 3 X 2 6	F 3 X 1 3	G 1 X 2 2	H 4 X 2 8
I 7 X 1 7	L 9 X 1 9	M 5 X 1 5	N 9 X 2 18
R 5 X 2 10	T 7 X 2 14	U 6 X 2 12	Y 8 X 2 16

Skill: multiplying by 1 and 2

Name ______________________________

A Happy Thought

S	H	A	R	E		A		C	H	O	C	O	L	A	T	E
10	16	6	12	4		6		18	16	9	18	9	8	6	7	4

M	A	L	T		W	I	T	H		M	E.
14	6	8	7		3	2	7	16		14	4

A 3×2 = 6	C 9×2 = 18	E 2×2 = 4	H 8×2 = 16
I 1×2 = 2	L 4×2 = 8	M 7×2 = 14	O 9×1 = 9
R 6×2 = 12	S 5×2 = 10	T 7×1 = 7	W 3×1 = 3

Name ______________________________

A Tongue Twister

B	E	A	S	T	I	E	S		B	L	O	W		B	I	G
0	6	10	9	12	2	6	9		0	5	1	7		0	2	4

B	L	U	E		B	U	B	B	L	E	S
0	5	3	6		0	3	0	0	5	6	9.

A: $5 \times 2 = $ 10	B: $0 \times 1 = $ 0	E: $6 \times 1 = $ 6	F: $7 \times 2 = $ 14
G: $4 \times 1 = $ 4	I: $2 \times 1 = $ 2	L: $5 \times 1 = $ 5	O: $1 \times 1 = $ 1
S: $9 \times 1 = $ 9	T: $6 \times 2 = $ 12	U: $3 \times 1 = $ 3	W: $7 \times 1 = $ 7

Name ______________________________

A Riddle
What is white on the outside, green on the inside, and hops?

A		F	R	O	G		S	A	N	D	W	I	C	H
3		24	14	8	6		18	3	15	0	9	12	27	21

A 1 X 3 3	C 9 X 3 27	D 0 X 3 0	F 8 X 3 24
G 2 X 3 6	H 7 X 3 21	I 4 X 3 12	N 5 X 3 15
O 4 X 2 8	R 7 X 2 14	S 6 X 3 18	W 3 X 3 9

Name ______________________________

Silly Seals

Write each product. Cross off the answer on the matching ball.

A.
5 x 3 = 15
1 x 3 = 3
6 x 3 = 18
3 x 3 = 9
9 x 3 = 27
0 x 3 = 0
4 x 3 = 12
2 x 3 = 6
8 x 3 = 24
7 x 3 = 21

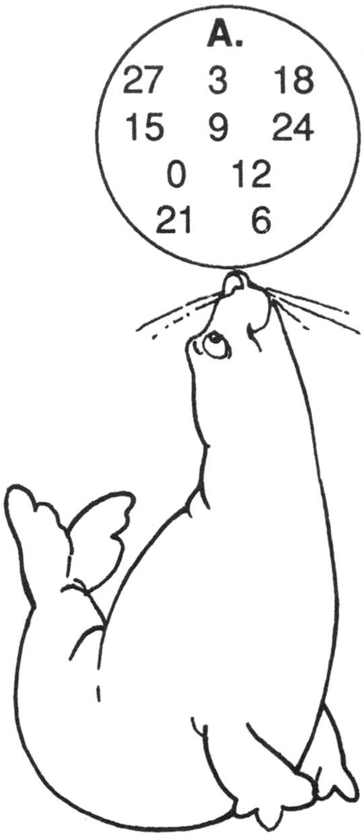

B.
9 x 4 = 36
3 x 4 = 12
8 x 4 = 32
7 x 4 = 28
0 x 4 = 0
4 x 4 = 16
6 x 4 = 24
1 x 4 = 4
5 x 4 = 20
2 x 4 = 8

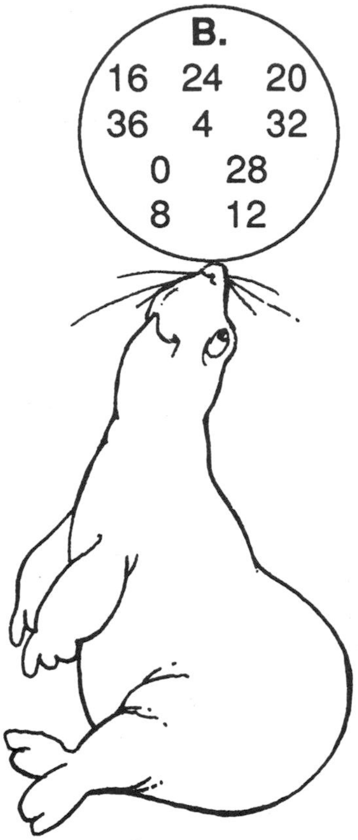

Solve each problem.

C. 3 x 8 = 24	**D.** 4 x 1 = 4	**E.** 3 x 9 = 27	**F.** 4 x 4 = 16	**G.** 3 x 5 = 15	**H.** 4 x 8 = 32
I. 3 x 6 = 18	**J.** 3 x 0 = 0	**K.** 4 x 5 = 20	**L.** 3 x 3 = 9	**M.** 4 x 9 = 36	**N.** 3 x 2 = 6
O. 4 x 3 = 12	**P.** 3 x 7 = 21	**Q.** 4 x 7 = 28	**R.** 4 x 6 = 24	 AWESOME!!	Score 36/36

Brainwork! Write three different multiplication facts whose answer is 12.

Name ____________________

A Riddle

I don't ask questions but you must answer me. What am I?

Oh ho!
Mystery Box

I		a	m		a		t	e	l	e	p	h	o	n	e
15		36	6		36		0	16	28	16	12	24	32	8	16

c	a	l	l
20	36	28	28

A 9 X 4 36	C 5 X 4 20	E 4 X 4 16	H 6 X 4 24
I 5 X 3 15	L 7 X 4 28	M 2 X 3 6	N 2 X 4 8
O 8 X 4 32	P 3 X 4 12	T 0 X 4 0	W 7 X 3 21

Name ______________________________

A Riddle
What pine has the sharpest needles?

A	n		A	n	g	r	y
6	28		6	28	15	24	16

P	o	r	c	u	p	i	n	e
18	33	24	20	0	18	36	28	2

A 3×2 = 6	C 5×4 = 20	E 1×2 = 2	G 5×3 = 15
I 9×4 = 36	N 7×4 = 28	O 11×3 = 33	P 9×2 = 18
R 8×3 = 24	U 0×3 = 0	Y 4×4 = 16	Z 9×3 = 27

Name ______________________________

Daffynition: Snowbank:

A		P	O	L	A	R		B	E	A	R
20		30	35	0	20	10		5	50	20	10

M	O	N	E	Y		B	A	N	K
55	35	40	50	15		5	20	40	25

A 4 X 5 = 20	**B** 1 X 5 = 5	**E** 10 X 5 = 50	**K** 5 X 5 = 25
L 0 X 5 = 0	**M** 11 X 5 = 55	**N** 8 X 5 = 40	**O** 7 X 5 = 35
P 6 X 5 = 30	**R** 2 X 5 = 10	**Y** 3 X 5 = 15	**Z** 9 X 5 = 45

Name ______________________________

A Tongue Twister

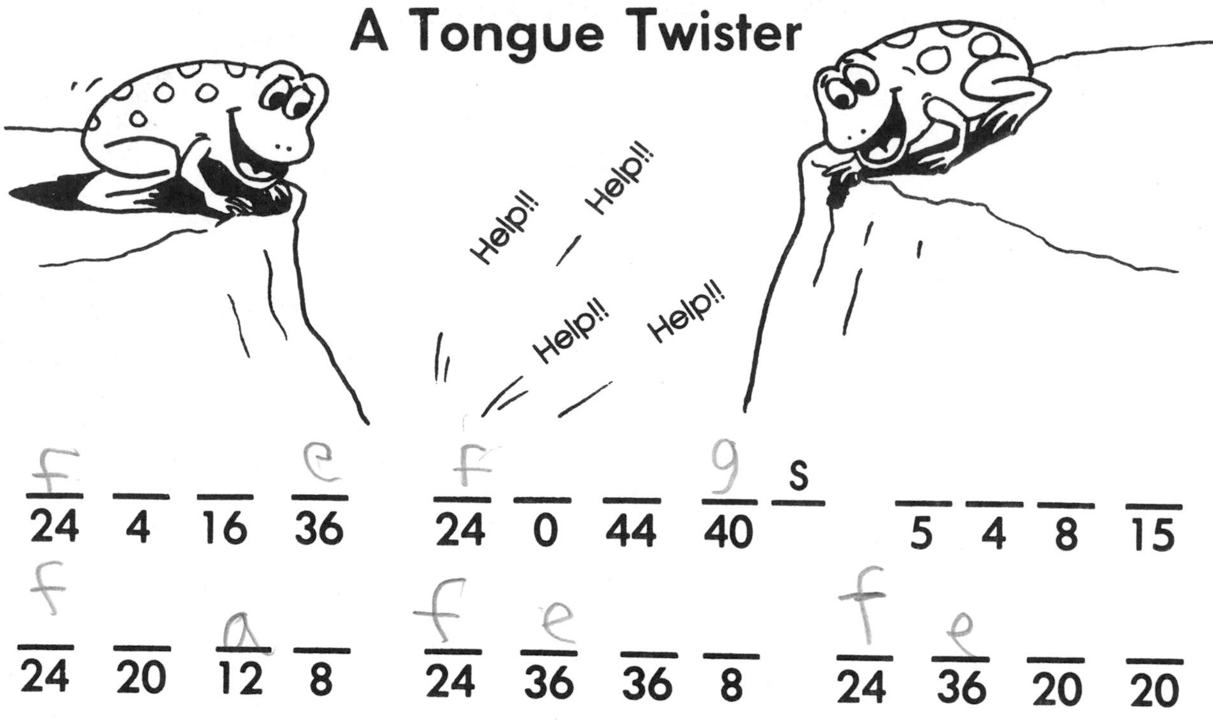

Help!!
Help!!
Help!!
Help!!

f			e		f			g	s					
24	4	16	36		24	0	44	40			5	4	8	15

f		a			f	e				f	e		
24	20	12	8		24	36	36	8		24	36	20	20

24	12	0.

A $3 \times 4 =$ 12	E $9 \times 4 =$ 36	F $6 \times 4 =$ 24	G $10 \times 4 =$ 40
H $3 \times 5 =$	I $1 \times 4 =$	L $4 \times 5 =$	O $11 \times 4 =$
R $0 \times 4 =$	T $2 \times 4 =$	V $4 \times 4 =$	W $1 \times 5 =$

Name ______________________________

A Riddle
How do you get an elephant out of a bottle?

__ __ __ __ __ __ __ __ __ __ __ __ __-
8 32 15 16   45 10 15   25 8 45 45 27 15

__ __ __ __ __ __ __ __ __ __!
32 8 40 21   10 24 9   8 40 45

B 5 X 5	E 3 X 5	H 2 X 5	I 6 X 4
L 9 X 3	M 3 X 3	N 4 X 4	O 2 X 4
P 8 X 4	R 7 X 3	T 9 X 5	U 10 X 4

Name ____________________

A Riddle
Why did the rocket lose its job?

. . . And what do I tell
my wife and
six little rockets?
?

__ __   __ __ __   __ __ __ __ __
24 42   18 12 54   36 24 6 48 30

__ __ __ __ __ y.
72 60 0 30 12

A 2 X 6	D 5 X 6	E 8 X 6	F 6 X 6
I 4 X 6	M 12 X 6	N 0 X 6	O 10 X 6
R 1 X 6	S 9 X 6	T 7 X 6	W 3 X 6

Name ____

A Happy Thought

Remember
that, son.

__ __ __ ’ __ __ __ __ __ __ __ __

0 18 30 48 0 48 42 6 12 54 48

__ __ __ __ __ __ __ __ __ __ __ __ __ !

48 60 66 12 24 0 36 36 12 6 12 30 48

A 9 X 6	B 11 X 6	D 4 X 6	E 2 X 6
F 6 X 6	G 7 X 6	I 0 X 6	N 5 X 6
O 10 X 6	R 1 X 6	S 3 X 6	T 8 X 6

Name ______________________ Skill: Multiplying by 5 and 6

Know-It-All Knights

Write each product. Cross off the answer on the matching shield.

A.
4 x 5 = ____
3 x 5 = ____
8 x 5 = ____
7 x 5 = ____
0 x 5 = ____
9 x 5 = ____
5 x 5 = ____
1 x 5 = ____
6 x 5 = ____
2 x 5 = ____

B.
3 x 6 = ____
1 x 6 = ____
6 x 6 = ____
5 x 6 = ____
9 x 6 = ____
0 x 6 = ____
7 x 6 = ____
2 x 6 = ____
8 x 6 = ____
4 x 6 = ____

Solve each problem.

C. 6 x 7	**D.** 5 x 8	**E.** 5 x 3	**F.** 6 x 4	**G.** 5 x 7	**H.** 6 x 5
I. 6 x 6	**J.** 6 x 0	**K.** 5 x 5	**L.** 6 x 9	**M.** 5 x 9	**N.** 5 x 1
O. 5 x 4	**P.** 6 x 8	**Q.** 5 x 7	**R.** 6 x 2		Score ____ / 36

Brainwork! If a number is multiplied by 5, the answer will always end in one of two numbers. Write the two numbers.

Name ______________________________

A Tongue Twister

If you want to catch big trout, you need the right bait . . .

___ ___ ___ ___   ___ ___ ___ ___ ___   ___ ___ ___ ___ ___
7 70 21 84   7 49 14 28 63   7 70 56 56 28

___ ___ ___ ___ ___ ___ ___ ___ ___ ___ ___ ___.
7 70 14 77 77 35 21 0 0 56 70 77

A 2×7	E 8×7	G 1×7	H 5×7
I 7×7	N 4×7	O 3×7	P 0×7
R 10×7	S 11×7	T 9×7	W 12×7

Skill: multiplying by 6 and 7

Name ______________________________

A Riddle
What do spooks eat for breakfast?

__ __ __ __ __   __ __ __ __ __ __ __ __
7 63 14 24 21   21 14 56 24 21 18 0 24

__ __ __   m __ __ __
56 30 35   18 12 49

A 8×7	D 5×7	E 0×7	G 1×7
H 9×7	I 3×6	K 7×7	L 2×6
N 5×6	O 2×7	S 4×6	T 3×7

Name ______________________________

A Riddle
If cows have horns.....

___ ___ ___   ___ ___ ___ ' ___   ___ ___ ___ ___
56 63 14   28 35 42 77   77 63 0 14

___ ___   ___ ___ ___ ___ - ___ ___ ___ ___ ?
21 35   7 0 0 49   7 0 0 49

B 1 X 7	D 4 X 7	E 0 X 7	G 3 X 7
H 9 X 7	N 6 X 7	O 5 X 7	P 7 X 7
T 11 X 7	W 8 X 7	Y 2 X 7	Z 10 X 7

Name ______________________________

Daffynition:

35 49 14 30 54 15 54 25 5 30 -

35   15 24 42 21 14   W   35 14 48 21 25 35 15

A 5×7	C 8×6	E 1×5	G 6×7
H 3×7	I 4×6	M 5×5	N 3×5
O 9×6	R 5×6	S 7×7	T 2×7

Name ______________________________

Skydiving

Write each product. Cross off the answer on the matching parachute.

A.
4 x 7 = ____
7 x 7 = ____
1 x 7 = ____
3 x 7 = ____
5 x 7 = ____
6 x 7 = ____
0 x 7 = ____
2 x 7 = ____
9 x 7 = ____
8 x 7 = ____

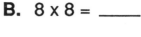

B.
8 x 8 = ____
3 x 8 = ____
0 x 8 = ____
7 x 8 = ____
4 x 8 = ____
1 x 8 = ____
6 x 8 = ____
9 x 8 = ____
2 x 8 = ____
5 x 8 = ____

Solve each problem.

C. 8 x 6	**D.** 7 x 1	**E.** 7 x 5	**F.** 8 x 4	**G.** 7 x 7	**H.** 8 x 8
I. 8 x 5	**J.** 8 x 0	**K.** 7 x 9	**L.** 8 x 3	**M.** 8 x 9	**N.** 7 x 2
O. 7 x 3	**P.** 7 x 8	**Q.** 8 x 2	**R.** 7 x 6	 Score ____ / 36	

Brainwork! Write a word problem that can be solved using this fact: 7 x 8 = 56

Name ____

A Riddle

What can you do if your pet monster hurts his toe?

__ __ __   __ __ __   __ __ __ __
80 0 8   24 72 88   24 72 16 16

__   __ __ __   (__ __ __)   __ __ __ __ __.
72   40 0 32   40 0 48   40 56 8 24 64

A 9×8	C 3×8	E 6×8	K 8×8
L 2×8	N 11×8	O 0×8	R 7×8
T 5×8	U 1×8	W 4×8	Y 10×8

Skill: multiplying by 9

Name ______________________________

A Riddle
Daffynition: Caterpillar

__   __ __ __ __   __ __   __   __ __ __
72   54 90 36 27   81 63   72   9 81 99

__ __ __ __ __ __ __
18 54 45 72 0 45 36

A 8×9	B 1×9	E 5×9	G 11×9
I 9×9	M 3×9	N 7×9	O 10×9
R 4×9	S 2×9	T 0×9	W 6×9

Name ______________________________

A Tongue Twister

__ __ __ __ __ __ __ __
45 16 54 0 40 18 18 48

__ __ __ __ __ __ __ __
45 18 56 0 9 18 36 36

__ __ __ __ __ __ __ __ __   __ __ __ __
45 32 0 18 45 9 32 18 36   45 9 18 24

__ __ __ __ .
45 56 36 40

A 8×7	E 2×9	F 5×9	I 4×8
L 1×9	N 6×8	O 2×8	R 0×8
S 4×9	T 5×8	U 6×9	W 3×8

Name ______________________________ Skill: Multiplying by 9 and 10

A Bright Bouquet

Write each product. Cross off the answer on the matching flowers.

A. 2 x 9 = ____

9 x 9 = ____

0 x 9 = ____

3 x 9 = ____

4 x 9 = ____

10 x 9 = ____

7 x 9 = ____

1 x 9 = ____

5 x 9 = ____

8 x 9 = ____

6 x 9 = ____

A.

B. 5 x 10 = ____

3 x 10 = ____

10 x 10 = ____

7 x 10 = ____

0 x 10 = ____

2 x 10 = ____

6 x 10 = ____

1 x 10 = ____

8 x 10 = ____

9 x 10 = ____

4 x 10 = ____

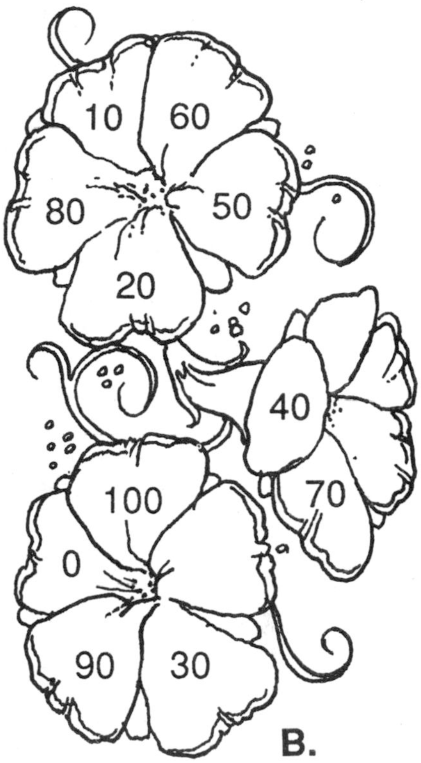

B.

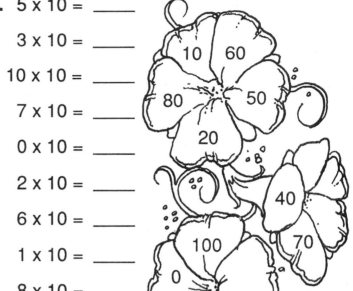

Solve each problem.

C. 9 x 9	**D.** 10 x 0	**E.** 9 x 3	**F.** 10 x 4	**G.** 9 x 8	**H.** 10 x 6
I. 9 x 6	**J.** 9 x 1	**K.** 10 x 5	**L.** 9 x 7	**M.** 10 x 9	**N.** 10 x 10
O. 10 x 3	**P.** 9 x 2	**Q.** 9 x 4	**R.** 10 x 8	 Score ____ 38	

Brainwork! Look at your answers for problems with 9 as a factor. If you add the digits in each answer, what number will you always get?

Name ______________________________

A Riddle

__ __ __ __   __ __ __ __ __ __
80 70 60 63   30 100 50 0 27 100

__ __ __ ' __   __ __ __ __ __
40 60 54 ' 63   30 100 50 0 27

__   __ __ __ ?   __
60   40 60 100 ?   60

__ __ __ __ __ __ __ __ __ __ __
10 40 100 27 80 30 100 50 0 27 100

A 6 X 10	C 4 X 10	D 3 X 10	E 3 X 9
H 7 X 10	I 5 X 10	N 6 X 9	R 10 X 10
S 1 X 10	T 7 X 9	V 0 X 10	W 8 X 10

Name ______________________________ Skill: Multiplying by 11 and 12

Dinosaur Duo

Write each product. Cross off the answer on the matching dinosaur.

A.

6 x 11 = _____
4 x 11 = _____
3 x 11 = _____
10 x 11 = _____
7 x 11 = _____
0 x 11 = _____
11 x 11 = _____

1 x 11 = _____
9 x 11 = _____
12 x 11 = _____
5 x 11 = _____
2 x 11 = _____
8 x 11 = _____

B.

5 x 12 = _____
3 x 12 = _____
10 x 12 = _____
8 x 12 = _____
6 x 12 = _____
12 x 12 = _____

4 x 12 = _____
0 x 12 = _____
7 x 12 = _____
9 x 12 = _____
11 x 12 = _____
1 x 12 = _____
2 x 12 = _____

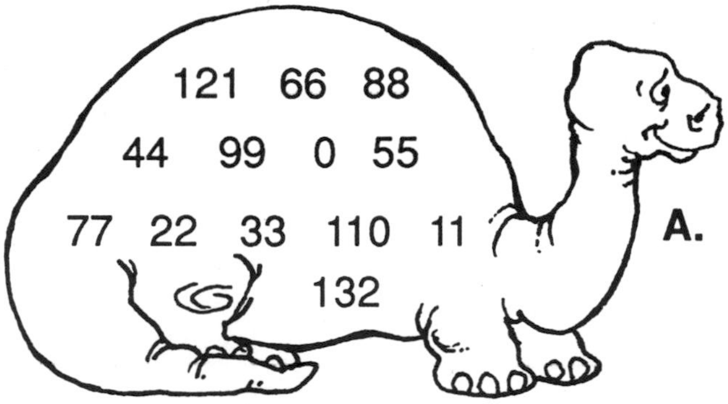

A.

B.

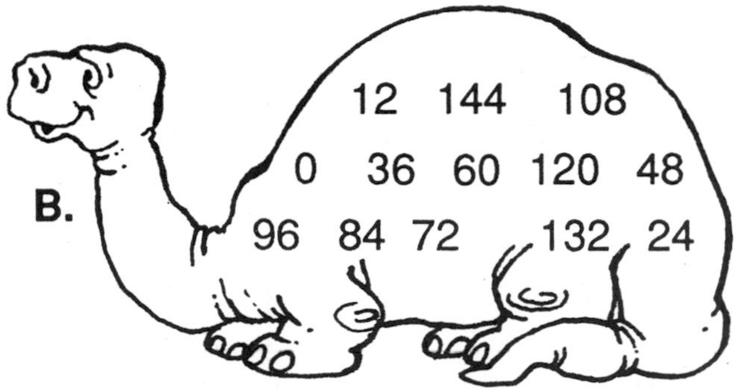

Solve each problem.

C. 12 x 3	**D.** 11 x 5	**E.** 12 x 12	**F.** 11 x 4	**G.** 12 x 6	**H.** 11 x 9
I. 12 x 2	**J.** 12 x 1	**K.** 11 x 11	**L.** 12 x 4	**M.** 11 x 0	**N.** 11 x 10
O. 11 x 7	**P.** 12 x 5	**Q.** 12 x 9	**R.** 11 x 8	 Score ____ / 42	

Brainwork! Write a multiplication word problem that uses the word *dozen*.

Name ______________________________ Skill: Multiplying by multiples of 10

Terrific Tens

Multiply.

A. 6 x 1 = _____

6 x 10 = _____

B. 3 x 4 = _____

3 x 40 = _____

C. 5 x 7 = _____

5 x 70 = _____

D. 8 x 2 = _____

8 x 20 = _____

E. 6 x 6 = _____

6 x 60 = _____

F. 9 x 6 = _____

9 x 60 = _____

G. 4 x 7 = _____

40 x 7 = _____

H. 8 x 5 = _____

8 x 50 = _____

I. 9 x 3 = _____

90 x 3 = _____

J. 7 x 3 = _____

7 x 30 = _____

K. 5 x 5 = _____

50 x 5 = _____

L. 7 x 0 = _____

70 x 0 = _____

M. 4 x 8 = _____

4 x 80 = _____

N. 3 x 6 = _____

30 x 6 = _____

O. 8 x 8 = _____

80 x 8 = _____

Solve each problem.

P. 20 x 9	**Q.** 20 x 3	**R.** 30 x 5	**S.** 40 x 4	**T.** 50 x 2	**U.** 90 x 9
V. 80 x 9	**W.** 70 x 7	**X.** 40 x 0	**Y.** 10 x 8		Score ___ / 40

Brainwork! Use these numbers (3, 4, 6, 8, 30, 40, 60, 80) to write four multiplication problems whose answer is 240.

Name ______________________________ Skill: Multiplying 2-digit by 1-digit numbers

Road Rally

Solve each problem by multiplying. Cross off the answer on the car.

		A. 24 x 2	B. 86 x 1	C. 13 x 3
		D. 20 x 4	E. 97 x 0	F. 14 x 2
G. 71 x 6	H. 63 x 3	I. 52 x 4	J. 91 x 5	K. 40 x 6
L. 82 x 3	M. 19 x 1	N. 22 x 2	O. 31 x 4	P. 60 x 7
Q. 41 x 8	R. 33 x 3	S. 92 x 4	T. 71 x 4	U. 52 x 3
V. 81 x 7	W. 72 x 3	X. 61 x 9	Y. 50 x 5	

Brainwork! If a car traveled the 52-mile Road Rally route four times, how many miles did it travel altogether?

Name ______________________________

Remember to **add** what you **carry**!

I call it regrouping!

Find the products.

23×3	37×4	95×2

38×2	86×5	27×3	49×2	65×4	18×5
46×3	20×4	49×2	52×7	93×8	72×6
19×7	38×8	64×6	42×9	80×5	24×7
48×7	15×9	36×8	57×7	19×9	60×7

Name ______________________ Skill: Multiplying 2-digit by 1-digit numbers, Regrouping

Fanciful Flight

Score ____ / 25

Solve each problem by multiplying.
Cross off the answer on the butterfly.

67
x 5
335

A. 19 x 2

B. 34 x 8

C. 63 x 9

D. 15 x 8

E. 49 x 5

F. 53 x 6

G. 27 x 4

H. 37 x 3

I. 28 x 7

J. 48 x 9

K. 65 x 3

L. 17 x 7

M. 88 x 2

N. 61 x 6

O. 86 x 8

P. 24 x 4

Q. 55 x 5

R. 31 x 9

S. 56 x 7

T. 36 x 3

U. 42 x 6

V. 93 x 4

W. 85 x 2

X. 39 x 7

Y. 19 x 8

Brainwork! If Dawn saw 13 butterflies and each had 6 spots on its wings, how many butterfly spots did she see?

Name ______________________________ Skill: Multiplying money by 1-digit numbers, Regrouping

Toy Store

Score ___ / 20

Solve each problem by multiplying. Cross off the answer on the list of receipts.

$1.75 x 6 = $10.50	A. $.71 x 8	B. $.25 x 4	C. $.36 x 5	D. $.42 x 3
E. $1.50 x 8	F. $6.00 x 6	G. $3.19 x 5	H. $5.82 x 6	I. $1.25 x 9
J. $8.09 x 9	K. $.57 x 7	L. $3.99 x 2	M. $6.17 x 4	N. $1.09 x 7
O. $7.08 x 3	P. $4.36 x 9	Q. $9.72 x 7		
R. $5.82 x 2	S. $8.04 x 8	T. $4.60 x 4		

Today's Receipts

$1.00	~~$10.50~~	$24.68
$1.26	$11.25	$34.92
$1.80	$11.64	$36.00
$3.99	$12.00	$39.24
$5.68	$15.95	$64.32
$7.63	$18.40	$68.04
$7.98	$21.24	$72.81

Brainwork! Sean is buying gifts for his three sisters. If he buys each of them a windmill bank, how much will he spend?

Happy Hundreds

Multiply.

A. 4 x 1 = ______

4 x 10 = ______

4 x 100 = ______

B. 7 x 3 = ______

7 x 30 = ______

7 x 300 = ______

C. 9 x 9 = ______

9 x 90 = ______

9 x 900 = ______

D. 5 x 6 = ______

50 x 6 = ______

500 x 6 = ______

E. 8 x 7 = ______

8 x 70 = ______

800 x 7 = ______

F. 6 x 2 = ______

60 x 2 = ______

6 x 200 = ______

G. 8 x 8 = ______

80 x 8 = ______

800 x 8 = ______

H. 4 x 5 = ______

4 x 50 = ______

4 x 500 = ______

Solve each problem.

I. 800 x 6	**J.** 900 x 4	**K.** 500 x 5	**L.** 300 x 8	**M.** 700 x 2	**N.** 400 x 6
O. 200 x 2	**P.** 400 x 8	**Q.** 600 x 7	**R.** 900 x 0	**S.** 300 x 6	**T.** 400 x 2
U. 100 x 7	**V.** 200 x 5	**W.** 600 x 9	**X.** 300 x 3		Score ___ / 40

Brainwork! Study the pattern above. Then solve these problems.

7 x 3,000 = ________ 9,000 x 8 = ________ 2 x 60,000 = ________

Name ____________________ Skill: Multiplying 3-digit by 1-digit numbers, Regrouping

Penguin Power

Solve each problem by multiplying.
Cross off the answer on the ice hole.

Score ____ / 25

126 x 3 = 378	A. 374 x 2	B. 151 x 9	C. 304 x 7	D. 519 x 4
E. 916 x 5	F. 573 x 6	G. 218 x 4	H. 835 x 8	I. 708 x 9
J. 709 x 7	K. 324 x 5	L. 783 x 3	M. 196 x 8	N. 186 x 6
O. 920 x 9	P. 934 x 4	Q. 492 x 6	R. 182 x 2	S. 582 x 7
		T. 307 x 8	U. 550 x 6	V. 954 x 3
		W. 875 x 5	X. 223 x 9	Y. 609 x 2

Brainwork! If 329 penguins were each flapping their two flippers, how many penguin flippers would be flapping?

Name ______________________________

258 × 2 = 16
Halt!
258 × 2 = 6
Go!
258 × 2 = 06
You forgot something!
258 × 2 = 116
Halt!
258 × 2 = 16
Go!
258 × 2 = 516
Success!

Find the products.

415×3	987×2	328×5	238×4	156×3
864×5	276×4	529×3	190×2	209×4
748×5	486×3	507×4	359×5	908×2
550×7	517×6	128×9	463×8	418×7
944×9	308×7	291×8	674×6	890×9
327×8	876×9	909×6	463×7	608×8

Name ______________________________ Skill: Multiplying 2-digit by 2-digit numbers, Regrouping

There She Blows!

Score ___ / 15

Solve by multiplying. Cross off the answer on the whale.

Example:

```
   67
 x 32
  134
 2010
2,144
```

A. 31 x 23

B. 90 x 58

C. 53 x 20

D. 71 x 46

E. 52 x 44

F. 82 x 64

G. 68 x 70

H. 94 x 42

I. 73 x 25

J. 59 x 66

K. 25 x 18

L. 41 x 96

M. 78 x 65

N. 18 x 78

O. 99 x 99

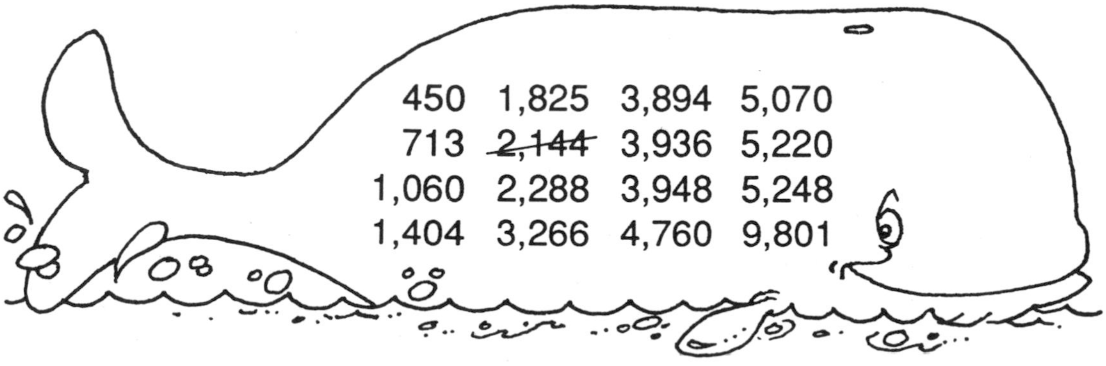

450	1,825	3,894	5,070
713	~~2,144~~	3,936	5,220
1,060	2,288	3,948	5,248
1,404	3,266	4,760	9,801

Brainwork! Solve these problems: 12 x 43 and 21 x 34. Which product is greater?

Name ______________________________

Example:
46
× 36
276
+ 1380
1656
You're in BIG trouble if you don't start your SECOND product with a ZERO!
Add the two products, and you're home free!

Multiply. Then add the products.

25 × 48	47 × 56	83 × 34	36 × 92	
42 × 49	50 × 87	71 × 58	63 × 79	38 × 29
56 × 33	84 × 25	27 × 54	93 × 26	78 × 57
45 × 37	67 × 88	72 × 39	83 × 50	46 × 74

Name ____________________

Multiply. Then add the products.

674 × 27	450 × 65	917 × 25	542 × 73	406 × 26
853 × 74	346 × 54	902 × 48	300 × 46	761 × 25
674 × 27	808 × 34	432 × 59	735 × 74	207 × 98
327 × 58	772 × 48	307 × 59	912 × 79	686 × 68

Name ______________________________

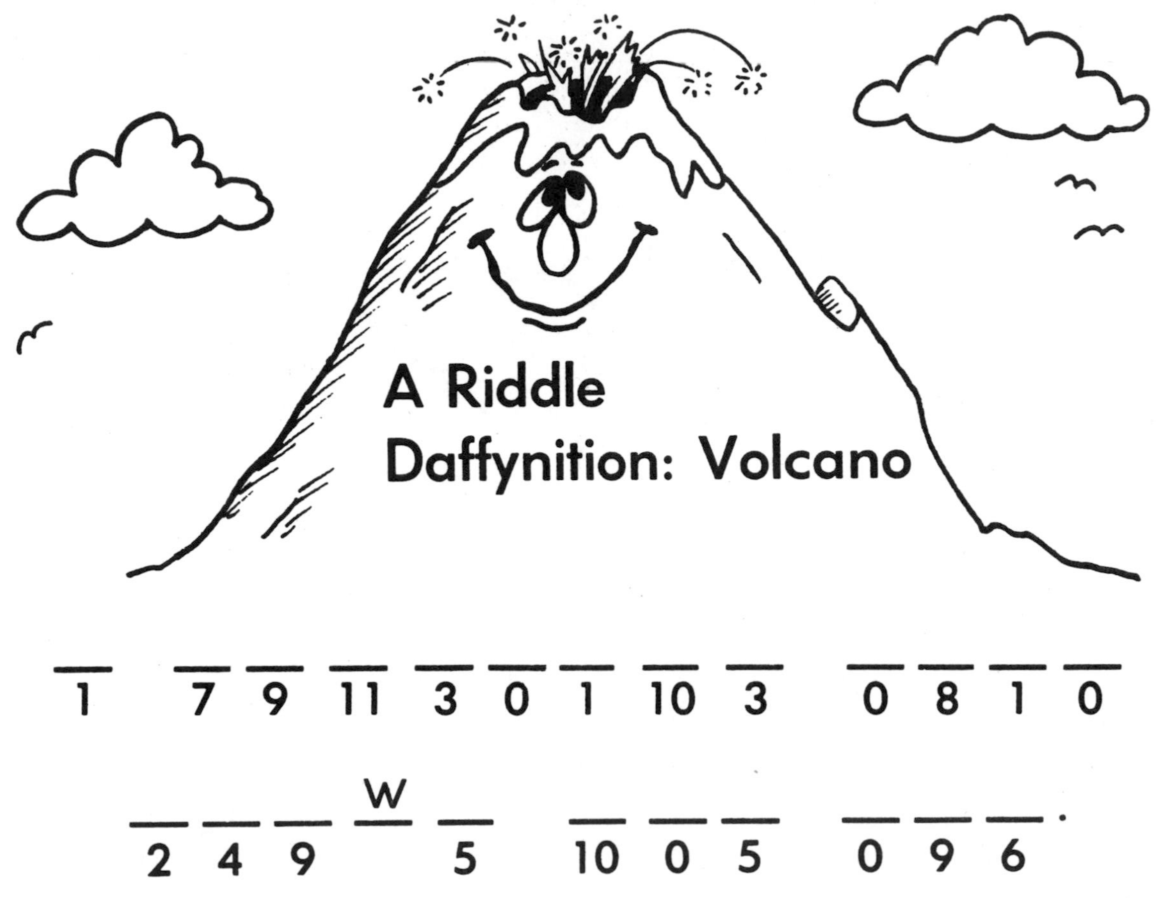

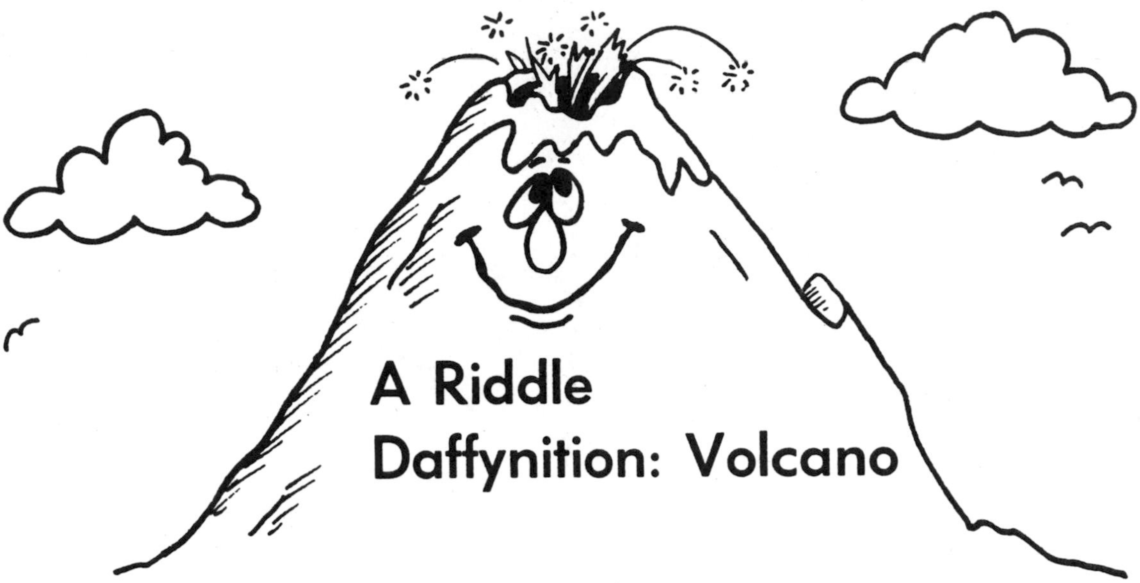

A Riddle
Daffynition: Volcano

__   __ __ __ __ __ __ __ __   __ __ __ __
1   7 9 11 3 0 1 10 3   0 8 1 0

__ __ __ W __   __ __ __   __ __ __.
2 4 9   5   10 0 5   0 9 6

A $1\overline{)1}$	B $2\overline{)4}$	H $2\overline{)16}$	I $1\overline{)10}$
L $2\overline{)8}$	M $1\overline{)7}$	N $3\overline{)9}$	O $2\overline{)18}$
P $2\overline{)12}$	S $2\overline{)10}$	T $3\overline{)0}$	U $1\overline{)11}$

Name ____________________

A Happy Thought

__ __ __ __' __   __ __ __
12 1 10 3 2   1 10 3

__ a __ __ __ __ __ __   __ __ __ __ __ __!
4   0 1 3 5 9 2   8 2 3 7 1 6

E $6 \div 3$ = 2	F $12 \div 3$ = 4	I $15 \div 3$ = 5	N $18 \div 3$ = 6
O $2 \div 2$ = 1	P $24 \div 3$ = 8	R $6 \div 2$ = 3	S $14 \div 2$ = 7
T $18 \div 2$ = 9	U $10 \div 1$ = 10	V $0 \div 2$ = 0	Y $12 \div 1$ = 12

Name ______________________________

A Riddle

The answer: a Roadhog
Then what's
the question?

___ ___ ___ ___   ___ ___ ___ ___ ___ ___   ___ ___ ___
10 2 8 1   8 0 9 6 8 4   2 8 3

___   ___ ___ ___?
8   5 8 7

A $2\overline{)16}$	C $3\overline{)15}$	C $2\overline{)10}$	H $1\overline{)2}$
I $2\overline{)18}$	L $3\overline{)12}$	M $2\overline{)12}$	N $1\overline{)0}$
R $2\overline{)14}$	S $3\overline{)9}$	T $2\overline{)2}$	W $1\overline{)10}$

Name ______________________________

A Happy Thought

___ ___ ___ ___   ___ ___ ___ ___ ___ ___ ___ ,
3 1 1 9   2 7 8 4 8 5 6

___ ___ ___ ___ ___   ___ ___ ___ !
2 12 9 1 0   3 8 10

D $1\overline{)10}$	E $3\overline{)3}$	G $3\overline{)18}$	I $3\overline{)24}$
K $3\overline{)9}$	L $3\overline{)12}$	M $3\overline{)21}$	N $3\overline{)15}$
P $3\overline{)27}$	R $1\overline{)0}$	S $3\overline{)6}$	U $1\overline{)12}$

Name ______________________________

A Tongue Twister

___   ___ ___ ___   ___ ___ ___   ___ ___ ___ ___ ___ ___
8   5 11 1   5 9 1   5 3 2 6 4 7

___ ___ ___ ___ ___   ___ ___ ___ ___ ___   ___ ___ ___ ___ ___.
5 3 2 4 6   5 4 10 4 0   5 4 8 9 5

A $4\overline{)32}$	D $4\overline{)24}$	E $4\overline{)16}$	H $1\overline{)11}$
I $4\overline{)8}$	L $4\overline{)36}$	N $3\overline{)0}$	P $4\overline{)12}$
R $4\overline{)28}$	S $4\overline{)20}$	V $1\overline{)10}$	Y $4\overline{)4}$

Name ______________________________

A Riddle
How do you make an elephant float?

__   S_ __ __ __ __   __ __
8   7 2 2 0   2 9

__ __ __ __ __ __ __ __ __   __ __ __ __ __ __ __ __
7 6 2 7 2 3 8 12 4   4 3 4 0 6 8 5 12

and   some   __ __ __ __   __ __ __ __
10 2 2 12   11 4 4 10

A $4\overline{)32}$	B $1\overline{)11}$	C $5\overline{)35}$	E $5\overline{)20}$
F $5\overline{)45}$	H $4\overline{)24}$	L $4\overline{)12}$	N $5\overline{)25}$
O $4\overline{)8}$	P $5\overline{)0}$	R $1\overline{)10}$	T $1\overline{)12}$

Name ______________________________

A Happy Thought
Yeah Yeah
Yeah!

___   ___ ___ ___ ___ ___ ___   ___ ___ ___ ___   ___ ___ ___

8   7 4 1 2 2 0   2 8 3 4   0 6 10

___ ___ ___ ___ ___.

9 6 5 1 0

A $6\overline{)6}$	D $6\overline{)30}$	E $6\overline{)24}$	I $6\overline{)48}$
K $6\overline{)18}$	L $5\overline{)10}$	O $5\overline{)30}$	R $6\overline{)42}$
T $5\overline{)45}$	U $5\overline{)50}$	Y $5\overline{)0}$	E $6\overline{)24}$

Name ______________________________

A Riddle

What did the ocean say when Superman flew over it?

__ __ __ __ i __ __ . l __ __ __ __ __

3 10 8 1 3 4 8 10 3 6 9

__ __ __ __ __ .

12 5 0 7 2

A $6\overline{)30}$	D $5\overline{)10}$	E $6\overline{)42}$	G $5\overline{)20}$
H $5\overline{)5}$	L $6\overline{)36}$	N $5\overline{)15}$	O $5\overline{)50}$
T $6\overline{)48}$	V $6\overline{)0}$	W $1\overline{)12}$	Y $6\overline{)54}$

Name ____

A Riddle

Riddle: Why are elephants so wrinkled?

_ _ _ _   _ _ _   _ _ _ _
4 1 0 5   12 9 8   5 0 5 6

_ _ _ _ _   _ _   _ _ _ _   _ _ _ ?
3 6 10 5 7   3 9   10 6 9 2   9 2 5

A $7\overline{)7}$	D $7\overline{)49}$	E $7\overline{)35}$	H $7\overline{)28}$
I $1\overline{)10}$	N $7\overline{)14}$	O $7\overline{)63}$	R $7\overline{)42}$
T $7\overline{)21}$	U $7\overline{)56}$	V $7\overline{)0}$	Y $1\overline{)12}$

Name ______________________________

A Riddle
What sheet can't
be washed?

a   ___ ___ ___ ___ ___   ___ ___   ___ ___ a ___ ___ ___ ___ ___
     3 4 7 7 8   0 5   11 6   9 9 2 10 1

___ a ___ ___ ___
9   9 7 6

E $7\overline{)49}$	F $7\overline{)35}$	G $6\overline{)6}$	H $7\overline{)28}$
I $6\overline{)12}$	N $1\overline{)10}$	O $6\overline{)0}$	P $7\overline{)63}$
R $7\overline{)42}$	S $7\overline{)21}$	T $7\overline{)56}$	W $1\overline{)11}$

Name ____________________

Hmmmmmmmmmm
FRED TUNA
832 Sea Way
Ocean Park

A Riddle
How do you send a letter to a fish?

__ __ __ __   __ __ __   __ __ S __   __   __ __ __ __.
9 10 6 12   11 3 8   5 2 3   7   4 2 1 8

A	D	E	F
$6\overline{)42}$	$6\overline{)54}$	$7\overline{)56}$	$7\overline{)35}$
H	**I**	**L**	**N**
$6\overline{)18}$	$7\overline{)14}$	$7\overline{)28}$	$6\overline{)6}$
O	**P**	**R**	**T**
$7\overline{)42}$	$6\overline{)72}$	$1\overline{)10}$	$7\overline{)77}$

Name ______________________________

DAFFYNITION: A Cactus

___   ___ ___ ___ ___ ___   ___ ___ ___ ___ ___ ___ ___ ___ ___ ___

1   7 5 1 2 0   10 5 2 4 3 8 6 5 9 2

A $5\overline{)5}$	C $6\overline{)24}$	G $7\overline{)49}$	H $6\overline{)36}$
I $6\overline{)30}$	N $5\overline{)10}$	O $7\overline{)63}$	P $5\overline{)50}$
S $7\overline{)56}$	T $6\overline{)0}$	U $5\overline{)15}$	W $5\overline{)55}$

Name ______________________________

Daffynition:

__ __ __ __ __ __ : __ __ __ __ __ __ __ __

9 2 4 10 4 5 : 2 0 3 9 9 4 6 8

__ __ __ __ __

1 9 2 7 6

A $8\overline{)16}$	D $8\overline{)64}$	E $8\overline{)48}$	G $7\overline{)7}$
I $8\overline{)32}$	N $7\overline{)35}$	O $7\overline{)21}$	P $7\overline{)49}$
R $8\overline{)72}$	S $1\overline{)10}$	W $8\overline{)0}$	Y $8\overline{)88}$

Name ______________________________

A Tongue Twister

__ __ __ __ __ __ __   __ __ __ __ __ __
3 8 4 12 10 0 7   6 4 5 3 8 2

__ __ __ __ __ __   __ __ __   __ __ __ __ __ __ __
3 5 3 3 8 2   7 5 9   6 4 5 3 8 2 1

__ __ __ __ __ __ __.
3 5 3 3 8 2 1

B $8\overline{)24}$	D $9\overline{)54}$	E $8\overline{)16}$	G $9\overline{)63}$
I $1\overline{)10}$	L $9\overline{)72}$	M $9\overline{)81}$	N $8\overline{)0}$
O $9\overline{)36}$	S $8\overline{)8}$	U $9\overline{)45}$	W $1\overline{)12}$

Name ______________________________

Riddle: What is gray and blue and is very heavy?

__   __ __ __ __
4   5 4 5 20

__ __ __ __ __ __ __ __
3 14 3 10 8 4 1 11

__ __ __ __ __ __ __   __ __ __
8 9 14 7 2 1 6   2 11 13

__ __ __ __ __ __
5 12 3 4 11 8

A $2\overline{)8}$	B $3\overline{)15}$	D $4\overline{)28}$	E $1\overline{)3}$	G $2\overline{)12}$
H $3\overline{)24}$	I $4\overline{)8}$	L $1\overline{)14}$	N $3\overline{)3}$	O $9\overline{)81}$
P $5\overline{)50}$	R $3\overline{)36}$	S $2\overline{)26}$	T $1\overline{)11}$	Y $2\overline{)40}$

Name ______________________________

How can you divide 19 apples equally among 9 boys?

Write each quotient and remainder.

r. : remainder

$\begin{array}{r} 2 \text{ r.}2 \\ 5\overline{)12} \end{array}$ $3\overline{)10}$

$2\overline{)17}$ $4\overline{)38}$

$4\overline{)33}$ $2\overline{)9}$

$3\overline{)23}$ $5\overline{)41}$

$2\overline{)11}$ $4\overline{)10}$

$4\overline{)25}$ $2\overline{)17}$

$5\overline{)33}$ $3\overline{)20}$

$3\overline{)28}$ $5\overline{)9}$

$4\overline{)29}$

Make applesauce, of course!

$6\overline{)14}$

$9\overline{)75}$ $8\overline{)75}$

$8\overline{)13}$ $6\overline{)50}$

$7\overline{)37}$ $9\overline{)89}$

$9\overline{)30}$ $8\overline{)30}$

$6\overline{)11}$ $7\overline{)19}$

$7\overline{)57}$ $6\overline{)55}$

$8\overline{)58}$ $8\overline{)66}$

$7\overline{)50}$ $7\overline{)48}$

$6\overline{)39}$ $9\overline{)46}$

$9\overline{)55}$ $6\overline{)33}$

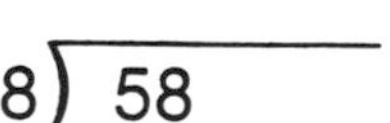

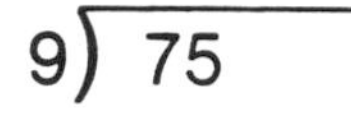

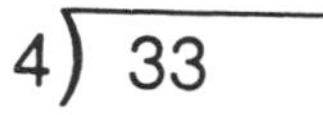

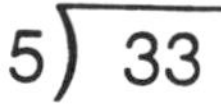

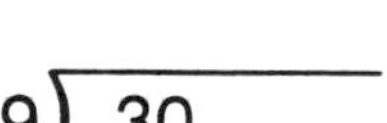

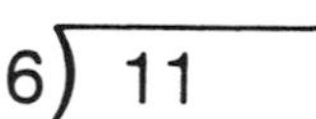

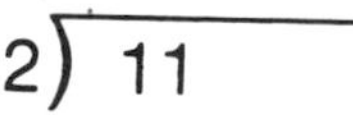

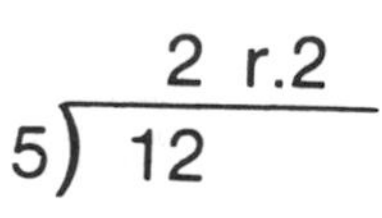

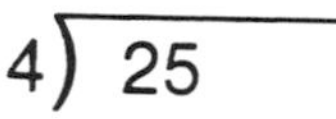

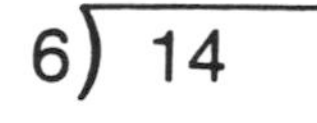

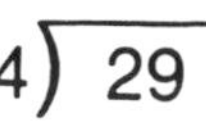

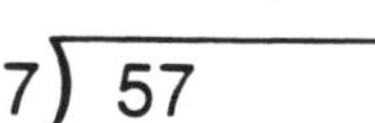

Name ______________________________

$\begin{array}{r} 36 \\ 2\overline{)72} \\ \underline{6} \\ 12 \\ \underline{12} \end{array}$	$8\overline{)96}$	$6\overline{)84}$	$7\overline{)91}$	$3\overline{)87}$
$2\overline{)74}$	$5\overline{)90}$	$7\overline{)84}$	$6\overline{)96}$	$5\overline{)75}$

Find the quotients and remainders.

$5\overline{)68}$	$2\overline{)71}$	$6\overline{)79}$	$7\overline{)94}$	$4\overline{)75}$
$3\overline{)74}$	$6\overline{)94}$	$3\overline{)47}$	$7\overline{)99}$	$6\overline{)88}$

Name ______________________________

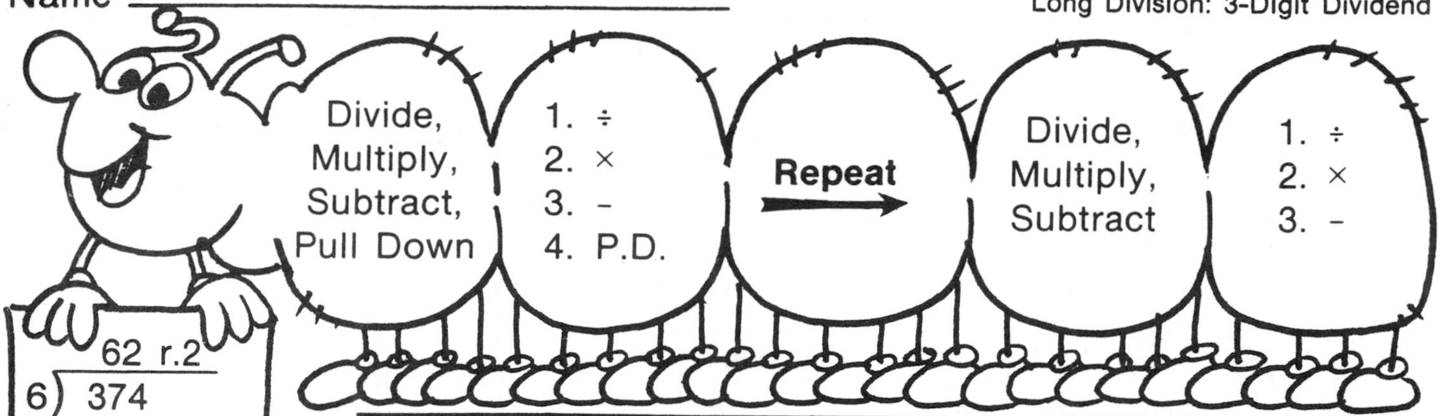

$$\begin{array}{r} 62 \text{ r.}2 \\ 6\overline{)374} \\ \underline{36} \\ 14 \\ \underline{12} \\ 2 \end{array}$$

Examples, Inc. !

Find the quotients.

	$9\overline{)756}$	$5\overline{)390}$	$7\overline{)196}$
$4\overline{)304}$	$3\overline{)201}$	$8\overline{)512}$	$6\overline{)222}$

Find the quotients and remainders.

$4\overline{)187}$	$8\overline{)339}$	$7\overline{)268}$	$3\overline{)176}$
$7\overline{)400}$	$6\overline{)215}$	$9\overline{)319}$	$4\overline{)107}$

Name ______________________________


```
     765 r. 4
6 ) 4594
    42
     39
     36
      34
      30
       4
```

Examples, Inc.

Find the quotients.

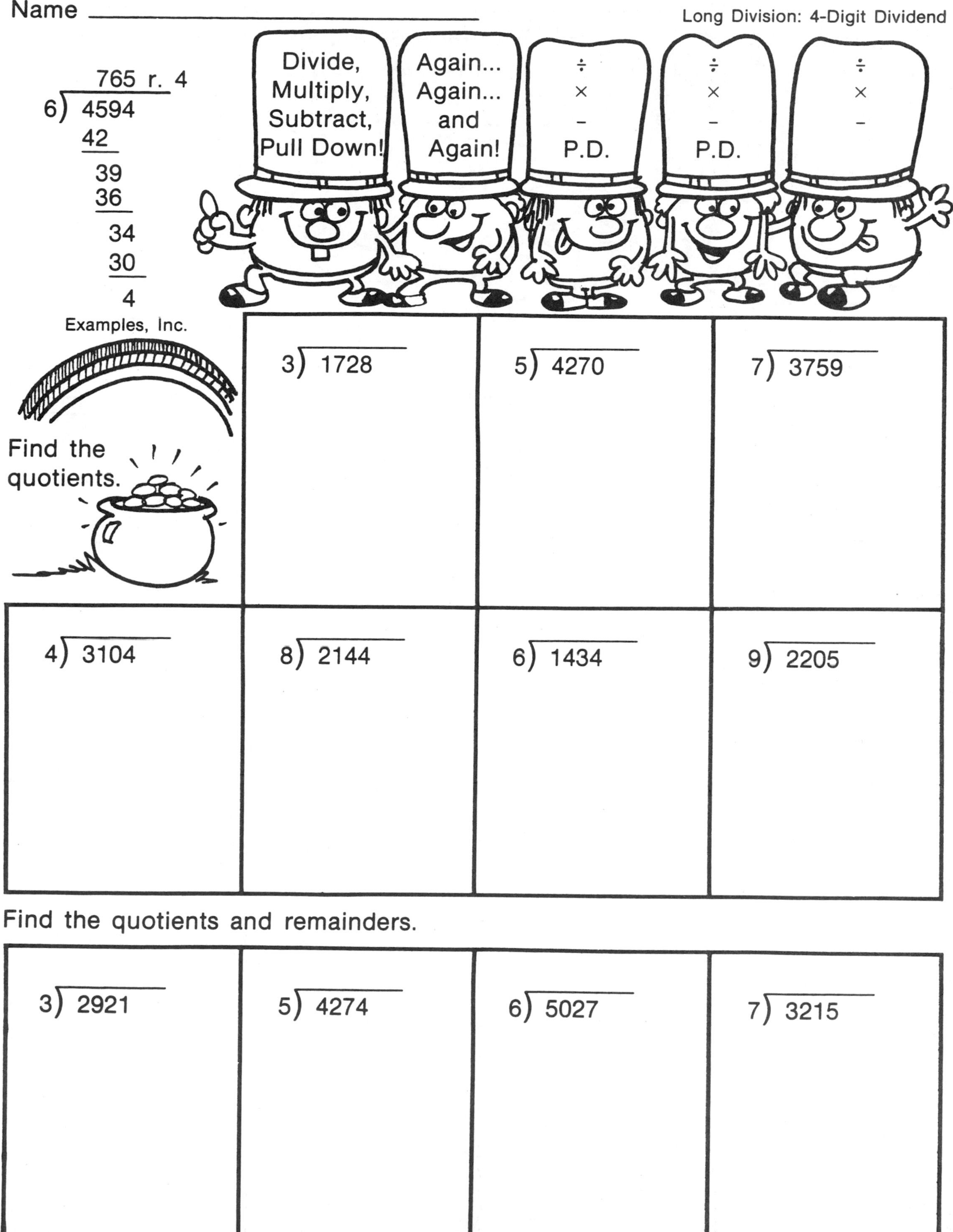

	$3\overline{)1728}$	$5\overline{)4270}$	$7\overline{)3759}$
$4\overline{)3104}$	$8\overline{)2144}$	$6\overline{)1434}$	$9\overline{)2205}$

Find the quotients and remainders.

$3\overline{)2921}$	$5\overline{)4274}$	$6\overline{)5027}$	$7\overline{)3215}$

Name ______________________

They don't make cars like they auto.

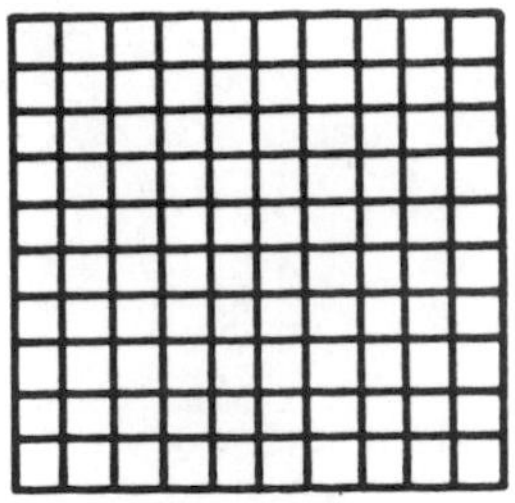

Shade .7

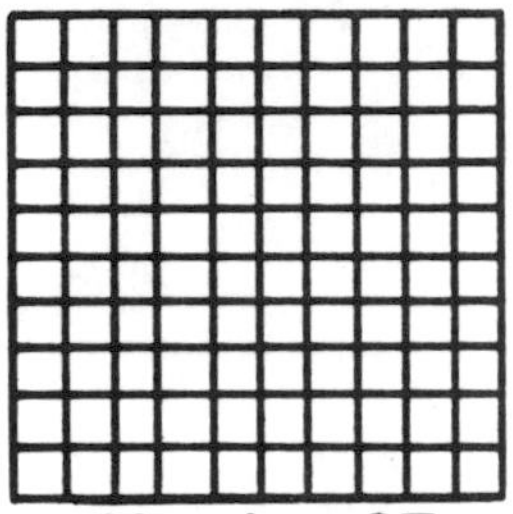

Shade .07

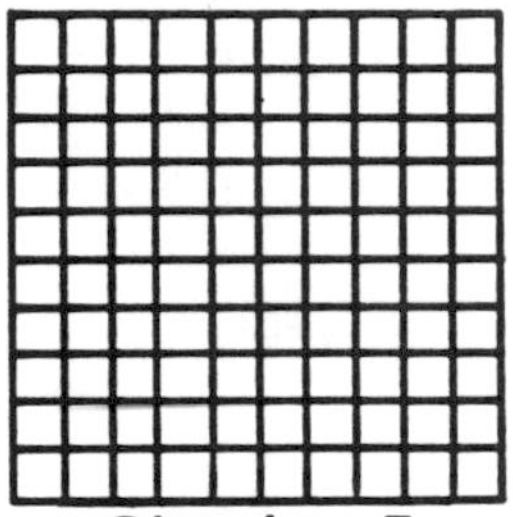

Shade .5

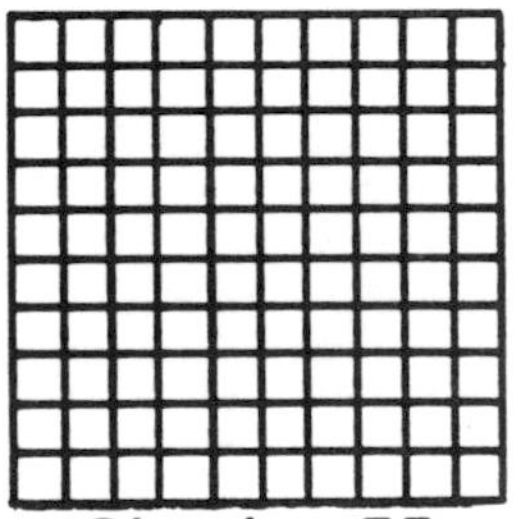

Shade .55

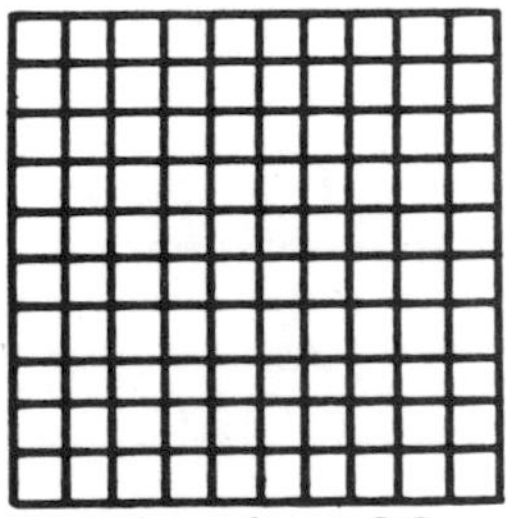

Shade .99

Write a decimal.

3 and 5 tenths ____ 6 and 5 tenths ____

5 hundredths ____ 35 hundredths ____

55 hundredths ____ 8 and 9 hundredths ____

2 and 1 hundredth ____ 25 and 2 tenths ____

$43\frac{6}{10}$ ________ $95\frac{3}{100}$ ________

$15\frac{9}{100}$ ________ $6\frac{25}{100}$ ________

$87\frac{18}{100}$ ________ $17\frac{2}{10}$ ________

$32\frac{5}{10}$ ________ $49\frac{8}{100}$ ________

$79\frac{1}{100}$ ________ $8\frac{4}{10}$ ________

$64\frac{4}{10}$ ________ $25\frac{55}{100}$ ________

$40\frac{4}{100}$ ________ $36\frac{9}{10}$ ________

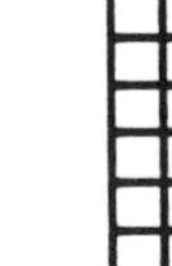

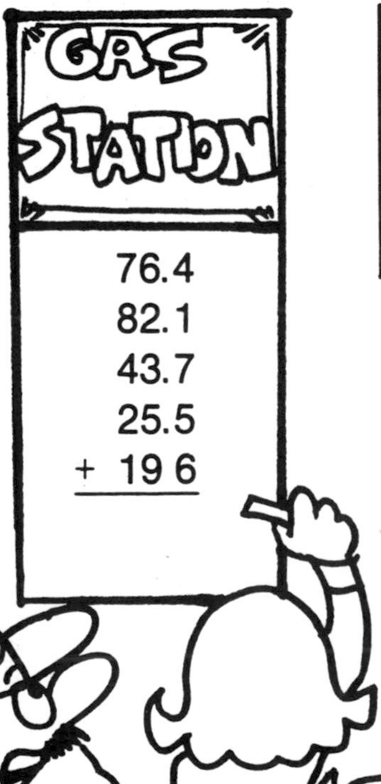
GAS STATION
76.4
82.1
43.7
25.5
+ 19 6

What if you left out the point?
That's a point to ponder!

Name ______________________________

Which way is the right way to write this problem? Circle A or B.

300.4 − 25.55 = ______

A. $\begin{array}{r} 300.4 \\ -\ 25.55 \\ \hline \end{array}$	**B.** $\begin{array}{r} 300.40 \\ -\ 25.55 \\ \hline \end{array}$

(see answer below)

Rewrite the following numbers to line up the decimal points, then add or subtract.

46.35 − 8.21	326.8 + 5.76	27.58 − 3.4
92.67 − 9.73	80.99 − 7.2	492.3 + 6.08
64.01 + 7.5	46.23 + 8.8	672.4 − 30.39
87.01 − 9.32	114.2 + 60.3 + 5.94 + 3.27	

Bravo for you if you circled B!

Name ______________________

What's your Common Sense I.Q.?

7¢ + 19¢ + $3.10 = $11.19 ◯ $3.19 ◯ $3.36 ◯

To make sense adding cents, change cent signs into decimals!

$ .07
.19
3.10

Rewrite the following figures in decimals; then add or subtract.

$15.50 - 75¢	$3.15 + 92¢	$2.05 - 58¢
$43.18 + 98¢	$300.00 - 69¢	$5.00 - 37¢

$72.75 + 6¢ + $5.50 + 93¢ + $200	$6.20 + 83¢ + $90 + 118.75

I can sense cents.
TREASURE CHEST
Since when?

Name ______________________________

CROSS-NUMERAL PUZZLE

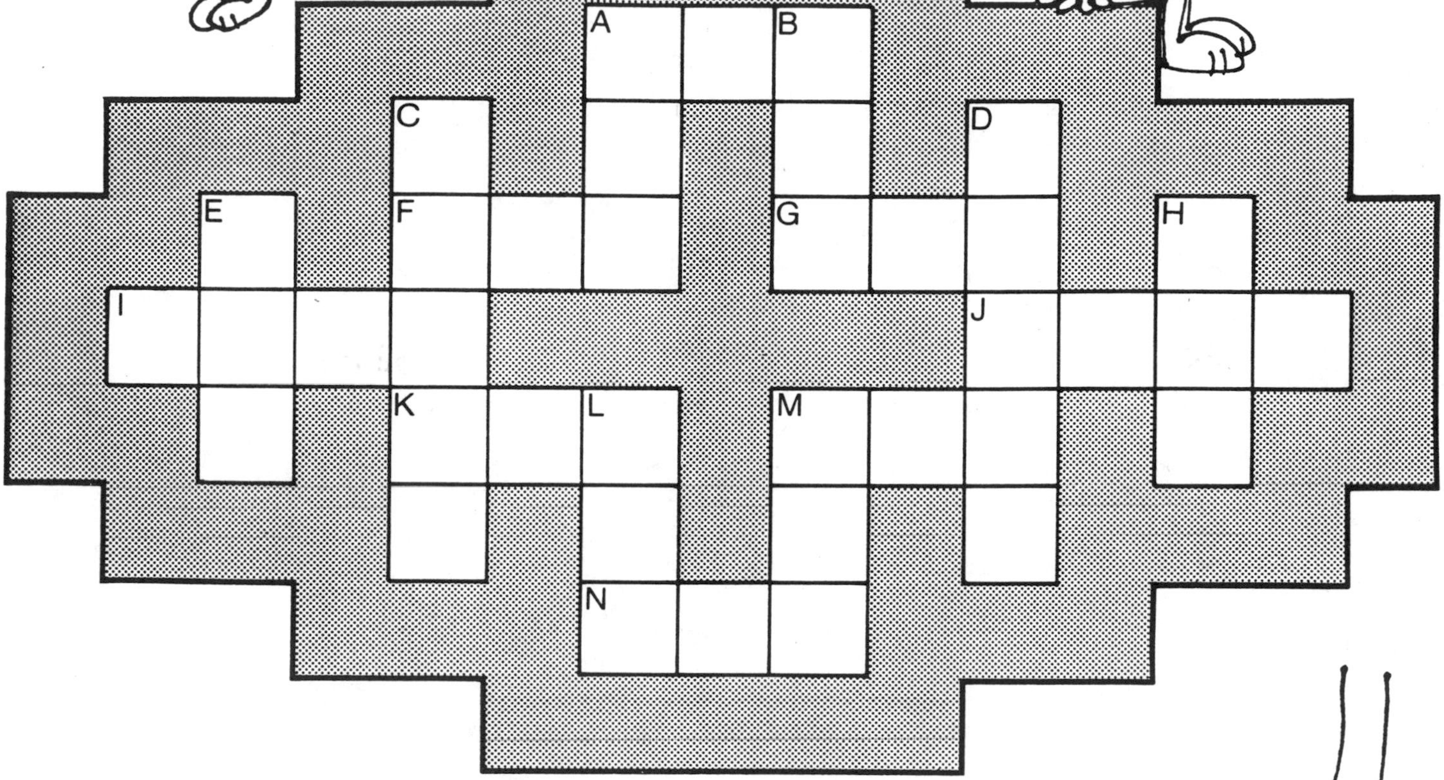

ACROSS

A. 465 + 372

F. 824 - 619

G. 700 - 215

I. 6,521 - 2,843

J. 2,774 + 984

K. 872 - 218

M. 198 + 258

N. 37 + 164

DOWN

A. 939 - 124

B. 658 + 96

C. 7,496 + 5,367

D. 8,064+ 7,296

E. 57 + 83 + 220

H. 29 + 68 + 353

L. 3,000 - 2,518

M. 219 + 212

Name ______________________________ Skill: Multiplying by 0, 1, 2, 3, and 4

Multiplication Backstroke

Multiply and write the answers.

Score ____ / 50

A. 2 x 5 = 10 1 x 3 = 3 0 x 9 = 0 1 x 2 = 2 0 x 2 = 0

B. 3 x 4 = 12 2 x 0 = 0 3 x 0 = 0 2 x 3 = 6 1 x 7 = 7

C. 0 x 5 = 0 4 x 4 = 16 3 x 7 = 21 0 x 0 = 0 4 x 5 = 20

D. 4 x 8 = 32 1 x 0 = 0 0 x 6 = 0 2 x 8 = 16 2 x 7 = 14

E. 4 x 2 = ____ 1 x 9 = ____

F. 1 x 5 = ____ 2 x 1 = ____

G. 1 x 4 = ____ 4 x 9 = ____ 4 x 1 = ____ 2 x 9 = ____ 3 x 8 = ____

H. 3 x 6 = ____ 3 x 5 = ____ 0 x 7 = ____ 4 x 0 = ____ 0 x 1 = ____

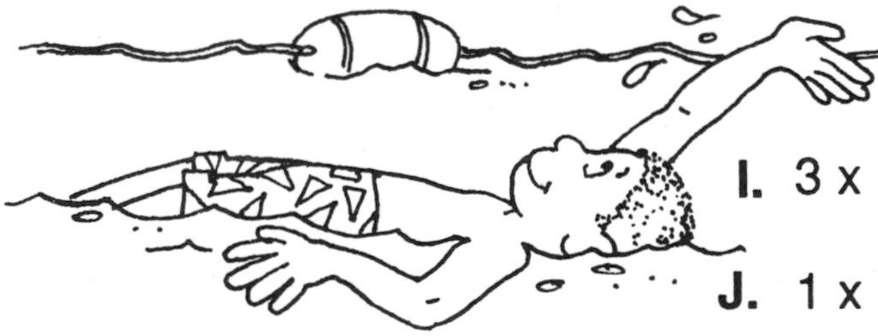

I. 3 x 1 = 3 0 x 3 = 0 4 x 6 = 24

J. 1 x 1 = 1 3 x 9 = 27 1 x 8 = 8

K. 4 x 7 = ____ 3 x 3 = ____ 2 x 6 = ____ 1 x 6 = ____ 0 x 8 = ____

L. 2 x 2 = ____ 2 x 4 = ____ 4 x 3 = ____ 0 x 4 = ____ 3 x 2 = ____

Brainwork! If Kara swims 9 laps four times a week, how many laps does she swim each week?

4x4 = 36

Name ______________________________ Skill: Multiplying by 5, 6, 7, 8, and 9

Kangaroo Fun

Multiply and write the answers.

A.

3 x 7 = ____
5 x 9 = ____
0 x 6 = ____
4 x 5 = ____
1 x 8 = ____
9 x 7 = ____
3 x 6 = ____
2 x 8 = ____
8 x 5 = ____
4 x 9 = ____

B.

6 x 8 = ____
8 x 9 = ____
5 x 6 = ____
1 x 5 = ____
4 x 7 = ____
0 x 9 = ____
8 x 6 = ____
3 x 5 = ____
7 x 7 = ____
9 x 8 = ____

C.

5 x 5 = ____
6 x 6 = ____
2 x 7 = ____
0 x 8 = ____
3 x 9 = ____
7 x 5 = ____
1 x 9 = ____
4 x 8 = ____
9 x 6 = ____
6 x 7 = ____

D.

7 x 6 = ____
0 x 5 = ____
9 x 9 = ____
1 x 7 = ____
3 x 8 = ____
7 x 9 = ____
2 x 5 = ____
8 x 7 = ____
5 x 8 = ____
2 x 6 = ____

E.

1 x 6 = ____
7 x 8 = ____
6 x 5 = ____
6 x 9 = ____
5 x 7 = ____
9 x 5 = ____
2 x 9 = ____
4 x 6 = ____
8 x 8 = ____
0 x 7 = ____

Brainwork! Write a word problem about kangaroos that can be solved using a multiplication fact from this page.

Name ______________________________

Busy Elves

These elves are making multiplication blocks. Solve the problems below. Then find out how many sides each block has by shading in the boxes with odd-numbered answers.

A.	5 x 5	1 x 3	9 x 7	6 x 5	9 x 5	9 x 8	1 x 7	2 x 2	2 x 9	4 x 7	9 x 3
B.	5 x 1	6 x 8	4 x 2	8 x 7	3 x 3	4 x 4	7 x 2	7 x 3	6 x 6	1 x 1	8 x 8
C.	7 x 9	3 x 1	9 x 3	9 x 4	7 x 7	3 x 2	8 x 3	5 x 8	9 x 9	2 x 5	4 x 6
D.	0 x 3	7 x 6	1 x 5	8 x 0	5 x 3	6 x 9	2 x 8	7 x 9	6 x 3	1 x 9	2 x 6
E.	5 x 7	5 x 9	3 x 5	8 x 4	9 x 1	3 x 4	7 x 1	0 x 0	6 x 2	5 x 4	3 x 9

Brainwork! Build your own block out of paper or clay. Write a multiplication fact on each side.

Name ____________________ Skill: Multiplication facts, 0–9 as factors

Tracking Down Facts

Write the missing factor or product.

A.

6 x ___ = 30
8 x 4 = ____
___ x 3 = 21
9 x ___ = 81
0 x 4 = ____
9 x 3 = ____
6 x ___ = 12
4 x 4 = ____
___ x 5 = 40
3 x ___ = 9

B.

3 x 8 = ____
5 x 4 = ____
___ x 3 = 0
8 x ___ = 8
2 x 7 = ____
___ x 5 = 25
6 x ___ = 54
6 x 4 = ____
7 x ___ = 42
3 x ___ = 12

C.

2 x 5 = ____
___ x 7 = 49
3 x ___ = 15
8 x 2 = ____
___ x 6 = 36
9 x ___ = 63
___ x 9 = 45
___ x 2 = 4
1 x 0 = ____
3 x 6 = ____

D.

2 x 4 = ____
___ x 7 = 7
6 x ___ = 48
8 x 5 = ____
___ x 1 = 3
5 x ___ = 35
___ x 9 = 72
___ x 2 = 6
7 x ___ = 28
8 x 8 = ____

E.

___ x 4 = 36
5 x ___ = 30
___ x 7 = 7
1 x ___ = 5
0 x 6 = ____
___ x 1 = 1
4 x ___ = 36
___ x 9 = 18
___ x 2 = 0
7 x 8 = ____

Score
____
50

Brainwork! Write four multiplication problems that have 7 as a missing factor.

Name ________________________________ Skill: Multiplication facts, 0–9 as factors

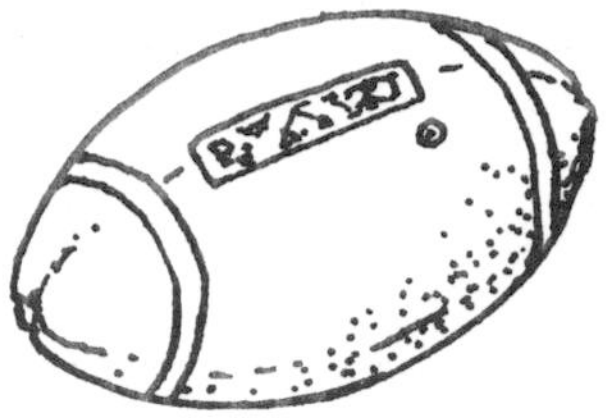

Football Fun

Solve by multiplying.

A.	8 x 5	5 x 3	6 x 1	0 x 0	4 x 9	1 x 2	3 x 7	9 x 2	8 x 9	2 x 9
B.	9 x 1	1 x 3	2 x 6	0 x 9	3 x 3	6 x 9	4 x 6	9 x 6	7 x 0	3 x 5
C.	6 x 3	0 x 3	5 x 1	4 x 1	9 x 0	6 x 2	2 x 7	5 x 2	1 x 4	7 x 6
D.	7 x 8	2 x 3	7 x 1	1 x 5	4 x 4	0 x 1	5 x 4	9 x 7	8 x 7	3 x 9
E.	8 x 1	1 x 1	6 x 6	5 x 9	3 x 0	6 x 7	4 x 7	3 x 8	6 x 0	9 x 5
F.	0 x 8	4 x 3	2 x 2	8 x 0	2 x 8	4 x 2	1 x 7	7 x 2	5 x 0	7 x 3
G.	1 x 8	6 x 4	3 x 1	2 x 0	8 x 8	0 x 4	5 x 5	3 x 2	9 x 4	7 x 5
H.	8 x 3	1 x 6	0 x 6	5 x 6	3 x 4	2 x 4	7 x 7	8 x 6	6 x 5	0 x 5
I.	6 x 8	9 x 3	2 x 1	4 x 0	4 x 8	0 x 2	5 x 7	9 x 2	1 x 0	7 x 9
J.	5 x 8	3 x 6	2 x 5	7 x 4	4 x 5	8 x 2	0 x 7	9 x 6	8 x 4	1 x 9

Brainwork! Write a football word problem that uses one of these multiplication facts.

Name ______________________________ Skill: Multiplication facts, 0–10 as factors

Beat the Clock!

A. Complete this chart by multiplying.

Example:

X	1	2
1	1	2
2	2	4

Can you finish it in five minutes or less?

Score ____
100

X	1	2	3	4	5	6	7	8	9	10
1										
2										
3										
4										
5										
6										
7										
8										
9										
10										

X	7	1	5	2	6	9	3	8	0	4
4										
9										
6										
1										
5										
8										
0										
3										
7										
2										

B. This multiplication chart is a little harder because the numbers are out of order.

Can you finish it in eight minutes or less?

Score ____
100

Name ____ Skill: Multiplication facts, 0–12 as factors

Multiplication Round-Up

Complete this chart by multiplying.

Example:

X	1	2
1	1	2
2	2	4

X	3	7	0	11	2	9	1	4	6	12	5	8	10
5													
9													
1													
6													
4													
12													
3													
10													
0													
8													
11													
2													
7													

Brainwork! Choose five facts you need to practice from this chart and write each one in two different ways. Example: 2 x 9 = 18   9 x 2 = 18

Name ______________________________

Skill: Review

Fill in the spaces only where 576 is the product.

66 × 6
9 × 63
282 × 2
313 × 2
7 × 88
6 × 93
156 × 4
9 × 84
273 × 2
4 × 164
13 × 22
8 × 82
6 × 96
86 × 7
154 × 4
192 × 3
12 × 34
288 × 2
12 × 36
33 × 17
64 × 9
144 × 4
71 × 6
72 × 8
94 × 6
156 × 3
28 × 28
12 × 48
62 × 8
64 × 8
13 × 33
14 × 34
19 × 28
24 × 24
16 × 36
66 × 6
76 × 8
18 × 32
86 × 7
23 × 25
76 × 6
26 × 26
86 × 6
212 × 3

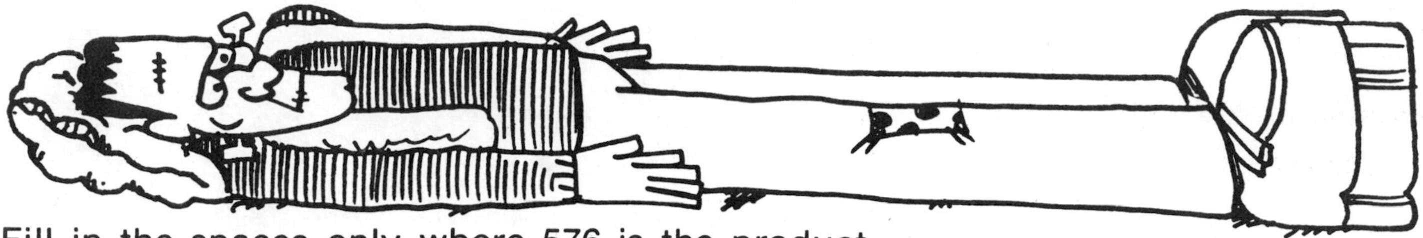

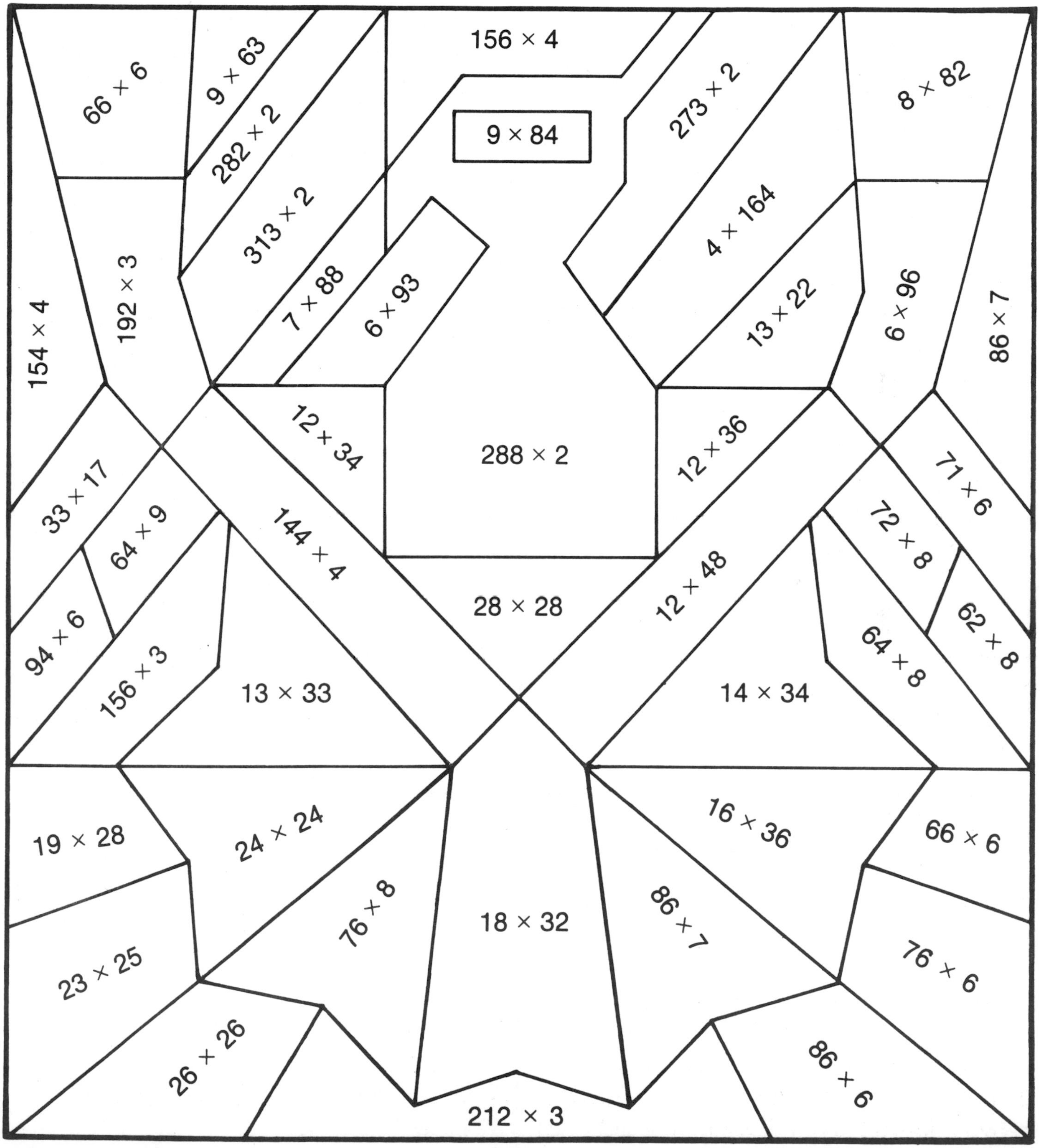

Name ______________________________ Skill: Review

When is a bright idea like a clock?

When ___ ___   ___ ___ ___ ___ ___ ___ ___   ___ ___ ___
1 2   3 4 5 6 7 8 9   10 11 12

Directions: Solve each division problem. Find the quotient and matching letter in the code box below to answer the riddle.

1. 4) 72	**2.** 3) 1458	**3.** 7) 161	**4.** 6) 2916
5. 2) 94	**6.** 9) 162	**7.** 5) 385	**8.** 4) 2756
9. 5) 115	**10.** 8) 464	**11.** 6) 150	**12.** 9) 6201

18	23	25	47	58	77	486	689
i	**s**	**n**	**r**	**o**	**k**	**t**	**e**

Name ____________________ Skill: Review

It's Magic

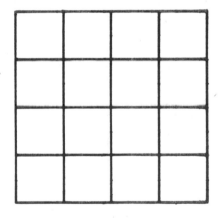

1. Find the missing numbers in this magic square. Four decimals in each row, column, and diagonal will give the same sum.

	.6	.7	1.7
.9	1.5	1.4	
	1.1	1.0	1.6
.8	1.8		.5

2. Add .7 to each number in the magic square you have just completed in problem **1**. See if you have made a new magic square!

3. Make your own magic squares using these numbers: 1.1, 1.3, 1.5, 1.7, 1.9, 2.1, 2.3, 2.5, 2.7

4. Make your own magic square using these numbers: 1.2, 1.4, 1.6, 1.8, 2.0, 2.2, 2.4, 2.6, 2.8

Name ______________________________

I. Add or Subtract.

1. $\begin{array}{r} 579 \\ +\ 364 \\ \hline \end{array}$

2. $\begin{array}{r} 24 \\ 31 \\ 68 \\ 59 \\ 32 \\ 40 \\ +\ 19 \\ \hline \end{array}$

3. $\begin{array}{r} 2367 \\ +\ 9684 \\ \hline \end{array}$

4. $\begin{array}{r} 815 \\ -\ 437 \\ \hline \end{array}$

5. $\begin{array}{r} 7500 \\ -\ 2864 \\ \hline \end{array}$

II. Multiply.

6. $\begin{array}{r} 48 \\ \times\ 3 \\ \hline \end{array}$

7. $\begin{array}{r} 395 \\ \times\ 6 \\ \hline \end{array}$

8. $\begin{array}{r} 72 \\ \times\ 49 \\ \hline \end{array}$

9. $\begin{array}{r} 283 \\ \times\ 67 \\ \hline \end{array}$

10. $\begin{array}{r} 704 \\ \times\ 58 \\ \hline \end{array}$

III. Divide.

11. $7\overline{)\ 44}$

12. $8\overline{)\ 30}$

13. $4\overline{)\ 72}$

14. $6\overline{)\ 2916}$

15. $5\overline{)\ 339}$

IV. Write a Decimal.

16. 4 and 3 tenths ______

17. 7 and 5 hundredths ______

Add or subtract.

18. 125.3 + 9.48

19. 417.6 − 36.25

20. \$5.20 + 85¢

SCORE	I	II	III	IV	TOTAL
					_____ × 5 = __________ %
Possible Right:	(5)	(5)	(5)	(5)	Possible Right: 20

Answer Key

Skill: 1 digit from 2 digit, no regrouping

Name ______________________________

Riddle: When should a battery call the doctor?

when it has a
72 11 91 52 | 86 58 | 11 33 25 | 33

bad attack
36 33 41 | 33 58 58 33 10 20

of acid
44 43 | 33 10 86 41

indigestion
86 52 41 86 60 91 25 58 86 44 52

A	B	C	D	E
36 − 3 = 33	39 − 3 = 36	13 − 3 = 10	46 − 5 = 41	98 − 7 = 91
F 48 − 5 = 43	**G** 66 − 6 = 60	**H** 15 − 4 = 11	**I** 88 − 2 = 86	**K** 29 − 9 = 20
N 58 − 6 = 52	**O** 49 − 5 = 44	**S** 28 − 3 = 25	**T** 59 − 1 = 58	**W** 79 − 7 = 72

Page 1

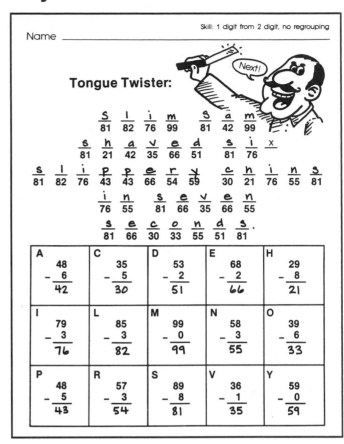

Skill: 1 digit from 2 digit, no regrouping

Name ______________________________

Tongue Twister:

slim sam
81 82 76 99 | 81 42 99

shaved six
81 21 42 35 66 51 | 81 76 x

slippery chins
81 82 76 43 43 66 54 59 | 30 21 76 55 81

in seven
76 55 | 81 66 35 66 55

seconds.
81 66 30 33 55 51 81

A	C	D	E	H
48 − 6 = 42	35 − 5 = 30	53 − 2 = 51	68 − 2 = 66	29 − 8 = 21
I 79 − 3 = 76	**L** 85 − 3 = 82	**M** 99 − 0 = 99	**N** 58 − 3 = 55	**O** 39 − 6 = 33
P 48 − 5 = 43	**R** 57 − 3 = 54	**S** 89 − 8 = 81	**V** 36 − 1 = 35	**Y** 59 − 0 = 59

Page 2

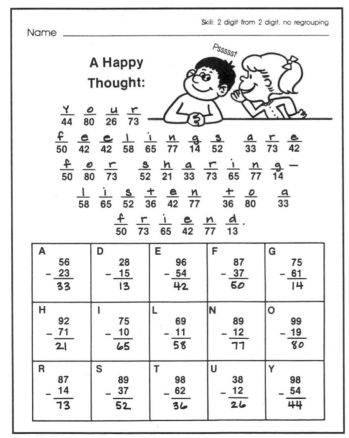

Skill: 2 digit from 2 digit, no regrouping

Name ______________________________

A Happy Thought:

your
44 80 26 73

feelings are
50 42 42 58 65 77 14 52 | 33 73 42

for sharing—
50 80 73 | 52 21 33 73 65 77 14

listen to a
58 65 52 36 42 77 | 36 80 | 33

friend.
50 73 65 42 77 13

A	D	E	F	G
56 − 23 = 33	28 − 15 = 13	96 − 54 = 42	87 − 37 = 50	75 − 61 = 14
H 92 − 71 = 21	**I** 75 − 10 = 65	**L** 69 − 11 = 58	**N** 89 − 12 = 77	**O** 99 − 19 = 80
R 87 − 14 = 73	**S** 89 − 37 = 52	**T** 98 − 62 = 36	**U** 38 − 12 = 26	**Y** 98 − 54 = 44

Page 3

Skill: 2 digit from 2 digit, no regrouping

Name ______________________________

A Daffynition:

reindeer—a cold
3 34 19 82 10 34 34 3 | 44 | 23 15 57 10

horse wearing a
63 15 3 25 34 | 2 34 44 3 19 82 30 | 44

television
0 34 57 34 58 19 25 19 15 82

antenna
44 82 0 34 82 82 44

A	C	D	E	G
76 − 32 = 44	84 − 61 = 23	97 − 87 = 10	55 − 21 = 34	72 − 42 = 30
H 88 − 25 = 63	**I** 79 − 60 = 19	**L** 89 − 32 = 57	**N** 98 − 16 = 82	**O** 25 − 10 = 15
R 75 − 72 = 3	**S** 65 − 40 = 25	**T** 15 − 15 = 0	**V** 99 − 41 = 58	**W** 83 − 81 = 2

Page 4

Answer Key

Name ____________________

Skill: 1 digit and 2 digit addends, regrouping

A Happy Thought:

Y o u   h a v e   a
100 53 84   82 40 25 31   40

s p e c i a l   s o n g
74 30 31 60 70 40 72   74 53 27 62

t o   s i n g — s i n g
55 53   74 70 27 62 — 74 70 27 62

o u t !
53 84 55

A: 31 + 9 = 40	C: 56 + 4 = 60	E: 25 + 6 = 31	G: 53 + 9 = 62	H: 74 + 8 = 82
I: 62 + 8 = 70	L: 66 + 6 = 72	N: 19 + 8 = 27	O: 46 + 7 = 53	P: 23 + 7 = 30
S: 65 + 9 = 74	T: 48 + 7 = 55	U: 79 + 5 = 84	V: 16 + 9 = 25	Y: 97 + 3 = 100

Page 5

Name ____________________

Skill: 2 digit addends, regrouping

A Tongue Twister:

B e a s t i e s
46 102 53 74 80 83 102 74

b i t e   b u n c h e s
46 83 80 102   46 95 50 55 90 102 74

o f   b a k e d
34 61   46 53 65 102 41

b u t t e r e d
46 95 80 80 102 70 102 41

b a n a n a s.
46 53 50 53 50 53 74

A: 17 + 36 = 53	B: 29 + 17 = 46	C: 27 + 28 = 55	D: 22 + 19 = 41	E: 63 + 39 = 102
F: 34 + 27 = 61	H: 32 + 58 = 90	I: 55 + 28 = 83	K: 29 + 36 = 65	N: 25 + 25 = 50
O: 15 + 19 = 34	R: 27 + 43 = 70	S: 48 + 26 = 74	T: 26 + 54 = 80	U: 66 + 29 = 95

Page 6

Name ____________________

Skill: 2 digit addends, regrouping

Riddle: What did Ben Franklin say when he discovered electricity?

B e n   w a s   t o o
53 71 61   57 84 67   50 42 42

s h o c k e d   t o
67 86 42 74 30 71 98   50 42

s a y   a n y t h i n g.
67 84 55   84 61 55 50 86 72 61 43

A: 58 + 26 = 84	B: 24 + 29 = 53	C: 45 + 29 = 74	D: 79 + 19 = 98	E: 23 + 48 = 71
G: 15 + 28 = 43	H: 67 + 19 = 86	I: 33 + 39 = 72	K: 15 + 15 = 30	N: 22 + 39 = 61
O: 27 + 15 = 42	S: 38 + 29 = 67	T: 25 + 25 = 50	W: 18 + 39 = 57	Y: 39 + 16 = 55

Page 7

Name ____________________

Skill: 2 digit addends, regrouping

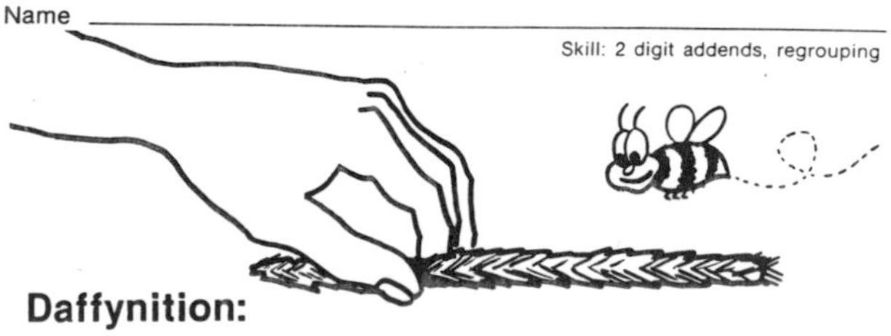

Daffynition:

p i p e c l e a n e r — a
77 52 77 85 96 134 85 60 91 85 40 — 60

t o o t h p i c k
31 63 63 31 82 77 52 96 45

w e a r i n g   a
62 85 60 40 52 91 73   60

s w e a t e r.
90 62 85 60 31 85 40

A: 24 + 36 = 60	C: 37 + 59 = 96	E: 57 + 28 = 85	G: 54 + 19 = 73	H: 49 + 33 = 82
I: 36 + 16 = 52	K: 28 + 17 = 45	L: 75 + 59 = 134	N: 52 + 39 = 91	O: 38 + 25 = 63
P: 18 + 59 = 77	R: 28 + 12 = 40	S: 73 + 17 = 90	T: 15 + 16 = 31	W: 43 + 19 = 62

Page 8

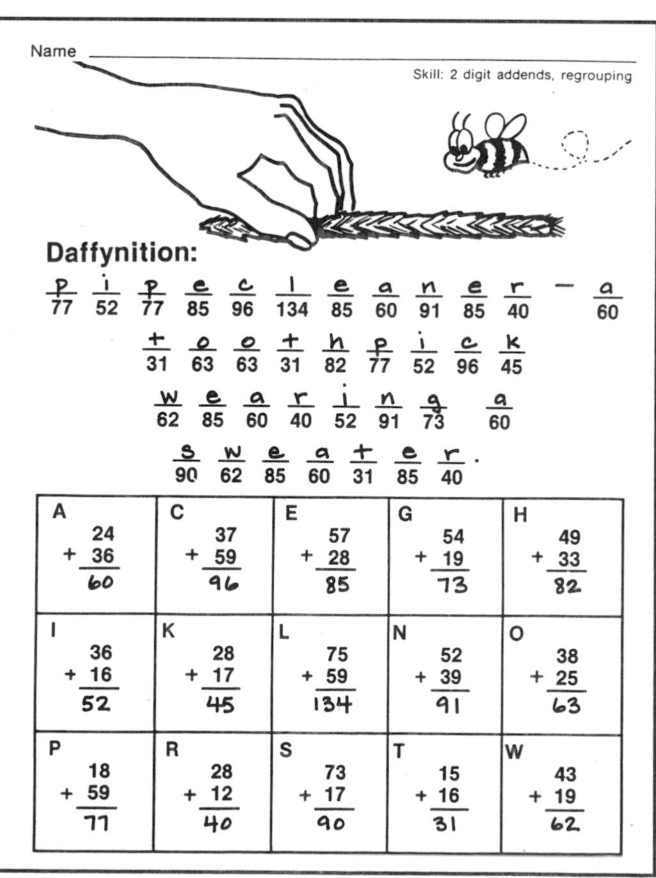

Answer Key

Name ______________________________

Skill: 2 digit addends, regrouping

Riddle: Why do elephants float on their backs?

t o k e e p t h e i r
47 100 58 54 54 68 47 75 54 32 30

s u n g l a s s e s
72 46 66 110 81 72 72 54 72

d r y .
31 30 93

D	E	G	H	I
17 + 14 = 31	39 + 15 = 54	55 + 55 = 110	36 + 39 = 75	16 + 16 = 32
K 29 + 29 = 58	**L** 22 + 59 = 81	**N** 37 + 29 = 66	**O** 56 + 44 = 100	**P** 49 + 19 = 68
R 15 + 15 = 30	**S** 23 + 49 = 72	**T** 29 + 18 = 47	**U** 18 + 28 = 46	**Y** 79 + 14 = 93

Page 9

Name ______________________________

Skill: 3 digit addends, no regrouping

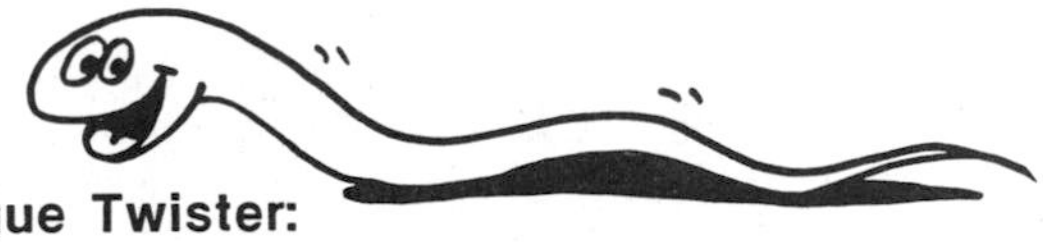

Tongue Twister:

s e v e n s i l v e r
698 587 339 587 739 698 949 483 339 587 509

s n a k e s
698 739 357 799 587 698

s l i t h e r e d
698 483 949 228 448 587 509 587 444

s l o w l y
698 483 299 593 483

s o u t h w a r d .
698 299 559 228 448 593 357 509 444

A	D	E	H	I
234 + 123 = 357	221 + 223 = 444	233 + 354 = 587	320 + 128 = 448	713 + 236 = 949
K 308 + 491 = 799	**L** 300 + 183 = 483	**N** 524 + 215 = 739	**O** 128 + 171 = 299	**R** 406 + 103 = 509
S 495 + 203 = 698	**T** 125 + 103 = 228	**U** 328 + 231 = 559	**V** 216 + 123 = 339	**W** 272 + 321 = 593

Page 10

Name ______________________________

Skill: 3 digit addends, no regrouping

Maybe I should get a cart.

Daffynition:

s h o p p e r — a
235 281 348 582 582 939 552 253

p e r s o n w h o
582 939 552 235 348 574 698 281 348

i s g o i n g t o
757 235 356 348 757 574 356 695 348

g o b u y — b u y .
356 348 467 279 266 467 279 266

A	B	E	G	H
142 + 111 = 253	362 + 105 = 467	125 + 814 = 939	121 + 235 = 356	150 + 131 = 281
I 421 + 336 = 757	**N** 421 + 153 = 574	**O** 236 + 112 = 348	**P** 450 + 132 = 582	**R** 121 + 431 = 552
S 135 + 100 = 235	**T** 352 + 343 = 695	**U** 146 + 133 = 279	**W** 153 + 545 = 698	**Y** 133 + 133 = 266

Page 11

Skill: 3 digit from 3 digit, no regrouping

Name ______________________________

A Tongue Twister:

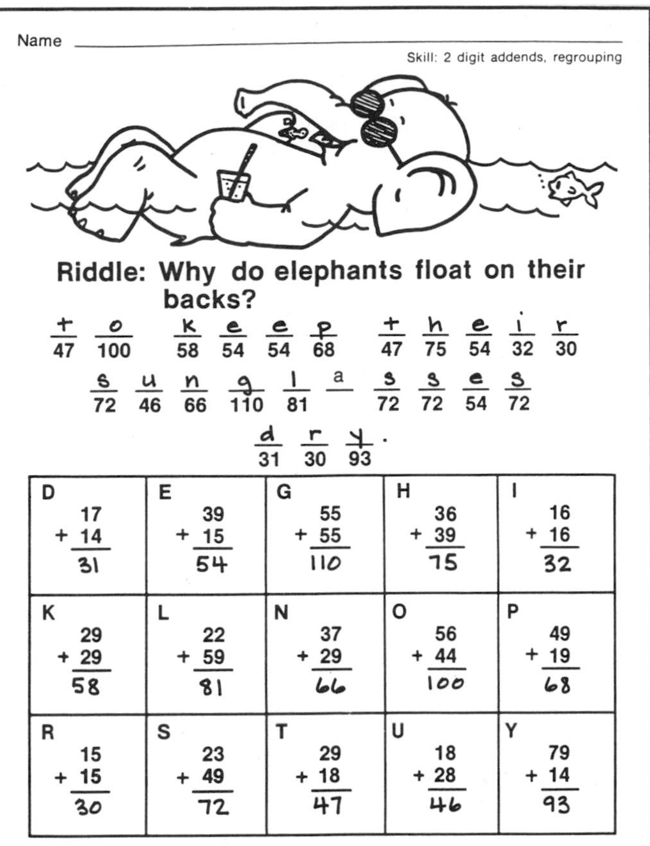

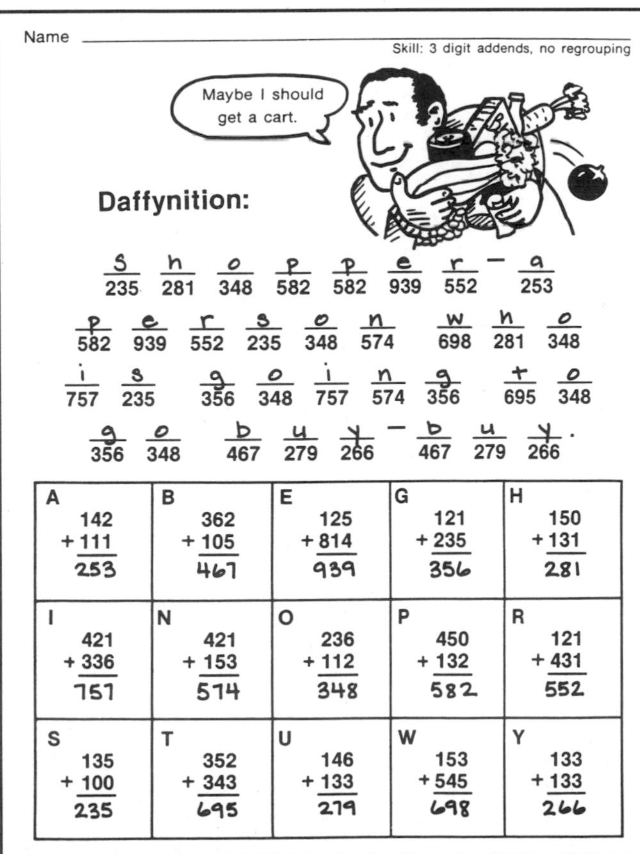

T h r e e
14 11 30 240 240

t e r r i b l e
14 240 30 30 633 453 400 240

t i g e r s t r i e d
14 633 141 240 30 8 14 30 633 240 312

t o t r a p t w o
14 4 14 30 424 202 14 570 4

t i n y t o a d s .
14 633 517 14 4 424 312 8

A	B	D	E	G
937 − 513 = 424	779 − 326 = 453	579 − 267 = 312	381 − 141 = 240	283 − 142 = 141
H 127 − 116 = 11	**I** 854 − 221 = 633	**L** 525 − 125 = 400	**N** 658 − 141 = 517	**O** 999 − 995 = 4
P 396 − 194 = 202	**R** 857 − 827 = 30	**S** 438 − 430 = 8	**T** 756 − 742 = 14	**W** 983 − 413 = 570

Page 12

Answer Key

Name ______________________ Skill: 3 digit from 3 digit, no regrouping

Happy Thought:

y o u n e e d b o t h
244 630 541 23 23 200 1 630 10 303

r a i n a n d
713 820 12 541 820 541 200

s u n s h i n e t o
474 541 474 303 12 541 23 10 630

m a k e a
736 820 340 23 820

r a i n b o w.
713 820 12 541 1 630 55

A 945 − 125 820	B 632 − 631 1	D 358 − 158 200	E 123 − 100 23	H 444 − 141 303
I 563 − 551 12	K 743 − 403 340	M 847 − 111 736	N 752 − 211 541	O 951 − 321 630
R 883 − 170 713	S 699 − 225 474	T 495 − 485 10	W 176 − 121 55	Y 367 − 123 244

Page 13

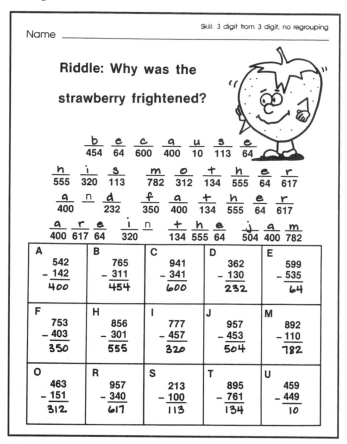

Name ______________________ Skill: 3 digit from 3 digit, no regrouping

Riddle: Why was the strawberry frightened?

b e c a u s e
454 64 600 400 10 113 64

h i s m o t h e r
555 320 113 782 312 134 555 64 617

a n d f a t h e r
400 232 350 400 134 555 64 617

a r e i n t h e j a m
400 617 64 320 134 555 64 504 400 782

A 542 − 142 400	B 765 − 311 454	C 941 − 341 600	D 362 − 130 232	E 599 − 535 64
F 753 − 403 350	H 856 − 301 555	I 777 − 457 320	J 957 − 453 504	M 892 − 110 782
O 463 − 151 312	R 957 − 340 617	S 213 − 100 113	T 895 − 761 134	U 459 − 449 10

Page 14

Name ______________________ Skill: 2 and 3 addends, regrouping

Riddle: The answer is a walkie-talkie.

But I don't think it's possible.

w h a t d o y o u
491 455 534 850 163 954 886 954

g e t w h e n y o u
660 730 850 491 455 730 571 886 954

c r o s s a
943 838 954 980 980 534

c e n t i p e d e
943 730 571 850 973 397 730 163 730

w i t h a r a d i o ?
491 973 850 455 534 838 534 163 973 954

A 418 + 116 534	C 724 + 219 943	D 128 + 35 163	E 414 + 316 730	G 25 + 635 660
H 39 + 416 455	I 349 + 624 973	N 524 + 47 571	O 427 + 527 954	P 289 + 108 397
R 519 + 319 838	S 127 + 853 980	T 811 + 39 850	W 28 + 463 491	Y 327 + 559 886

Page 15

Name ______________________ Skill: 2 and 3 digit addends, regrouping to 10's

A Happy Thought:

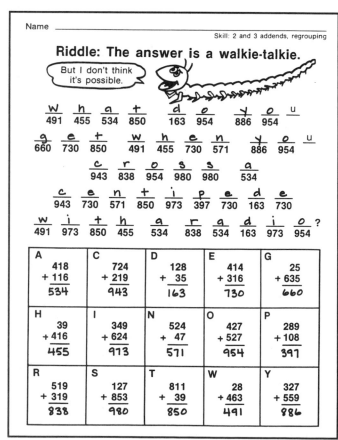

Are you out there?

H e l l o t o a l l
858 576 973 973 442 634 442 150 973 973

t h e f r i e n d s
634 858 576 662 790 371 576 357 83 732

I ' v e y e t t o
371 638 576 972 576 634 634 442

m e e t !
64 576 576 634

A 113 + 37 150	D 46 + 37 83	E 529 + 47 576	F 18 + 644 662	H 29 + 829 858
I 126 + 245 371	L 427 + 546 973	M 29 + 35 64	N 109 + 248 357	O 228 + 214 442
R 447 + 343 790	S 416 + 316 732	T 419 + 215 634	V 219 + 419 638	Y 143 + 829 972

Page 16

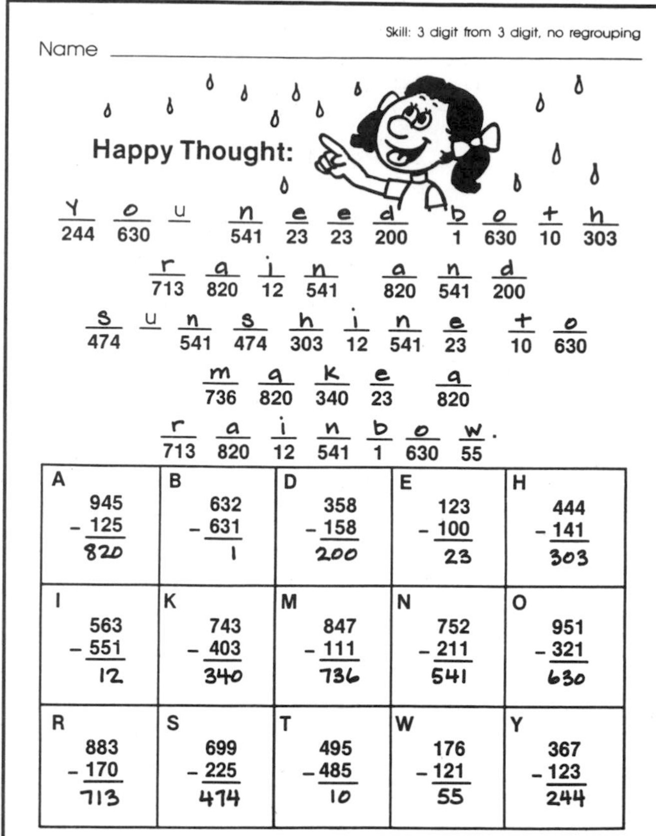

Answer Key

Name ____________________

Skill: 3 digit addends, regrouping to 10's

Happy Thought:

y o u ' r e m y
643 440 588 554 560 781 643

b e s t f r i e n d,
242 560 485 324 953 554 278 560 670 250

s u p e r k i d!
485 588 591 560 554 795 278 250

B 123 + 119 242	D 143 + 107 250	E 422 + 138 560	F 839 + 114 953	I 159 + 119 278
K 456 + 339 795	M 362 + 419 781	N 456 + 214 670	O 315 + 125 440	P 282 + 309 591
R 216 + 338 554	S 108 + 377 485	T 107 + 217 324	U 469 + 119 588	Y 426 + 217 643

Page 17

Name ____________________

Skill: 3 digit addends, regrouping to 10's

Although marmalade
is good too.

Riddle:

W h a t d o s h e e p
433 788 235 686 361 482 433 535 535 420

s p r e a d o n
482 420 853 535 788 686 361 380

t h e i r t o a s t ?
235 433 535 894 853 235 361 788 482 235

L a m b j a m.
923 788 483 451 490 788 483

A 369 + 419 788	B 142 + 309 451	D 268 + 418 686	E 429 + 106 535	H 109 + 324 433
I 287 + 607 894	J 321 + 169 490	L 609 + 314 923	M 158 + 325 483	N 264 + 116 380
O 236 + 125 361	P 305 + 115 420	R 409 + 444 853	S 223 + 259 482	T 129 + 106 235

Page 18

Name ____________________

Skill: 3 digit addends, regrouping to 10's

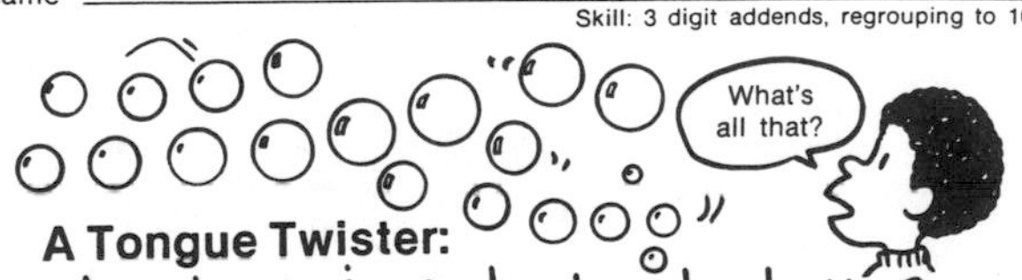
What's
all that?

A Tongue Twister:

A b r i g h t b l u e
652 890 666 593 785 950 793 890 394 212 371

b r o n t o s a u r u s
890 666 991 874 793 991 442 652 212 666 212 442

b l e w b i l l i o n s
890 394 371 910 890 593 394 394 593 991 874 442

o f b r o w n
991 668 890 666 991 910 874

b u b b l e s.
890 212 890 890 394 371 442

A 436 + 216 652	B 771 + 119 890	E 157 + 214 371	F 529 + 139 668	G 358 + 427 785
H 845 + 105 950	I 164 + 429 593	L 207 + 187 394	N 525 + 349 874	O 185 + 806 991
R 538 + 128 666	S 223 + 219 442	T 558 + 235 793	U 109 + 103 212	W 705 + 205 910

Page 19

Name ____________________

Skill: 2 and 3 digit addends, regrouping to 100's

Riddle: What did the highway say to the street?

I can't hear anything!

"I h a v e t h a t
600 509 317 269 984 623 509 317 623

t i r e d,
623 600 916 984 635

r u n d o w n
916 709 438 635 506 257 438

f e e l i n g."
429 984 984 236 600 438 935

A 153 + 164 317	D 462 + 173 635	E 591 + 393 984	F 274 + 155 429	G 743 + 192 935
H 251 + 258 509	I 390 + 210 600	L 193 + 43 236	N 258 + 180 438	O 235 + 271 506
R 334 + 582 916	T 362 + 261 623	U 80 + 629 709	V 176 + 93 269	W 163 + 94 257

Page 20

Answer Key

Name ______________________

Skill: 2 and 3 digit addends, regrouping to 100's

Tongue Twister:

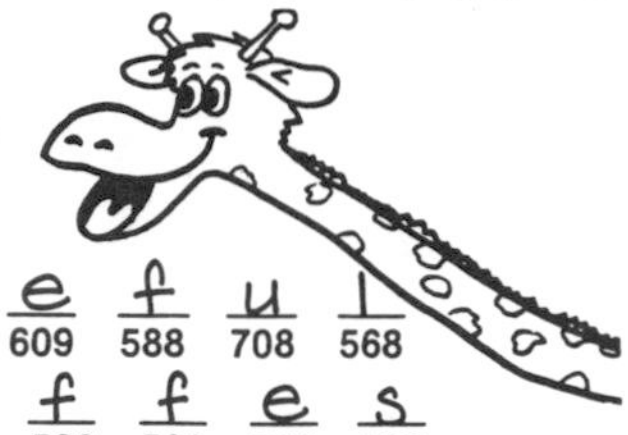

Graceful — 924 647 450 406 609 588 708 568

giraffes — 924 616 647 450 588 588 609 938

graze — 924 647 450 306 609 on — 576 227

gigantic — 924 616 924 450 227 840 616 406

grapes. — 924 647 450 829 609 938

A 260 + 190 = 450	C 150 + 256 = 406	E 532 + 77 = 609	F 397 + 191 = 588	G 462 + 462 = 924
I 240 + 376 = 616	L 287 + 281 = 568	N 173 + 54 = 227	O 386 + 190 = 576	P 648 + 181 = 829
R 573 + 74 = 647	S 767 + 171 = 938	T 450 + 390 = 840	U 346 + 362 = 708	Z 113 + 193 = 306

Page 21

Name ______________________

Skill: 3 digit addends, regrouping to 100's

A Happy Thought:

The — 222 409 627 best — b 627 609 222 part — 258 377 524 222

of — 329 767 you — 436 329 648 is — 500 609 who — 217 409 329

you — 436 329 648 are — 377 524 627

inside. — 500 849 609 500 938 627

A 283 + 94 = 377	D 777 + 161 = 938	E 296 + 331 = 627	F 483 + 284 = 767	H 156 + 253 = 409
I 170 + 330 = 500	N 279 + 570 = 849	O 246 + 83 = 329	P 165 + 93 = 258	R 372 + 152 = 524
S 492 + 117 = 609	T 161 + 61 = 222	U 394 + 254 = 648	W 141 + 76 = 217	Y 385 + 51 = 436

Page 22

Name ______________________

Skill: 3 digit addends, regrouping to 100's

Riddle: Why do monsters forget?

Everything — 929 612 929 944 534 627 605 988 934 867

goes — 867 504 929 643 in — 988 934 one — 504 934 929

ear — 929 807 944 and — 807 934 339

out — 504 510 627 the — 627 605 929

other — 504 627 605 929 944 six. — 643 988 745

A 343 + 464 = 807	D 166 + 173 = 339	E 299 + 630 = 929	G 585 + 282 = 867	H 451 + 154 = 605
I 293 + 695 = 988	N 583 + 351 = 934	O 292 + 212 = 504	R 793 + 151 = 944	S 350 + 293 = 643
T 493 + 134 = 627	U 130 + 380 = 510	V 351 + 261 = 612	X 453 + 292 = 745	Y 343 + 191 = 534

Page 23

Name ______________________

Skill: 3 digit addends, regrouping to 10's and 100's

A Happy Thought:

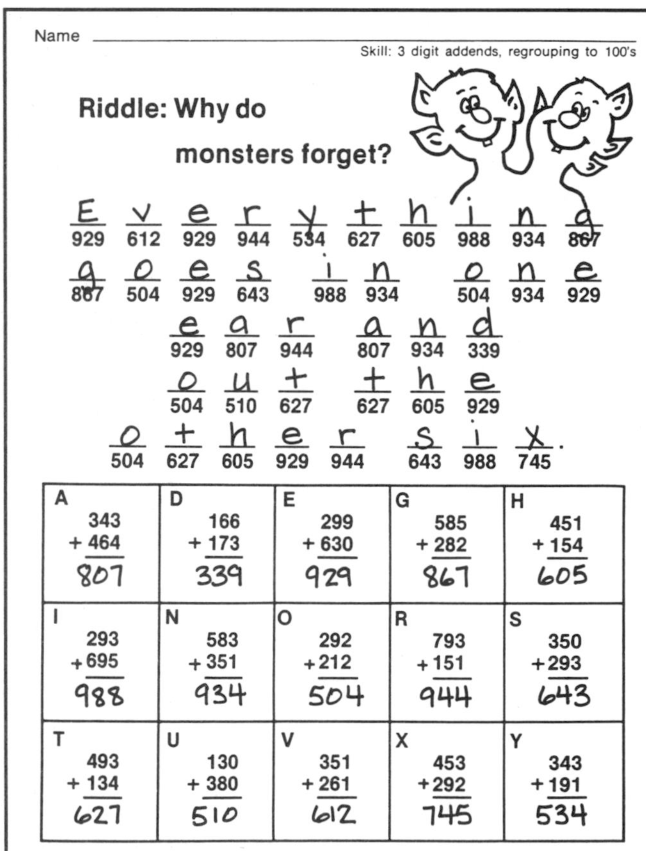

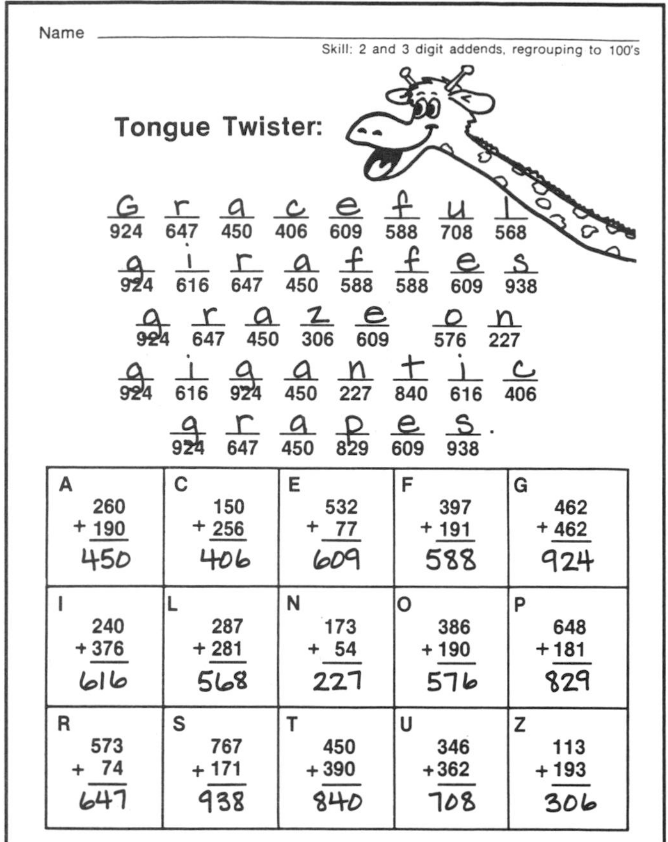

You — 627 730 697 just — j 697 870 641 won — 913 730 304

the — 641 405 531 "Super — 870 697 653 531 711

Kid" — 500 820 706 award. — 427 913 427 711 706

A 199 + 228 = 427	D 459 + 247 = 706	E 387 + 144 = 531	H 228 + 177 = 405	I 443 + 377 = 820
K 394 + 106 = 500	N 189 + 115 = 304	O 543 + 187 = 730	P 469 + 184 = 653	R 243 + 468 = 711
S 285 + 585 = 870	T 342 + 299 = 641	U 346 + 351 = 697	W 534 + 379 = 913	Y 399 + 228 = 627

Page 24

Answer Key

Name ____________________ 3-4 Digit Addition

Find the sums.

286 + 302 = 588			6235 + 2644 = 8,879
623 + 748 = 1,371	584 + 309 = 893	7489 + 6306 = 13,795	4928 + 7058 = 11,986
782 + 857 = 1,639	350 + 695 = 1,045	7085 + 7164 = 14,249	2343 + 6785 = 9,128
275 + 859 = 1,134	845 + 296 = 1,141	9428 + 9195 = 18,623	2683 + 7970 = 10,653
394 + 785 = 1,179	402 + 698 = 1,100	2975 + 7186 = 10,161	9462 + 3389 = 12,851

Page 25

Name ____________________ Column Addition

Find the sums.

- 6, 4, 9, 2, 8, 3, 7, + 1 = 40
- 8, 3, 2, 7, 5, + 6 = 31
- 2, 5, 8, 9, 3, + 5 = 32
- 6, 3, 9, 4, 2, + 8 = 32
- 37, 48, 93, + 66 = 244
- 852, 694, 481, + 738 = 2,765
- 37, 86, 92, + 23 = 238
- 3, 5, 9, 1, 2, 6, + 7 = 33
- 43, 28, + 56 = 127
- 54, 96, + 35 = 185
- 8, 4, 2, 7, 6, 3, + 9 = 39

Page 26

Name ____________________ Skill: 2 digit from 2 digit, regrouping

A Tongue Twister:

F(18) r(16) o(48) w(4) n(22) i(58) n(22) g(37) F(18) r(16) a(57) n(22)
f(18) o(48) u(12) n(22) d(79) f(18) i(58) f(18) t(36) e(29) e(29) n(22)
f(18) a(57) t(36) f(18) l(9) y(66) i(58) n(22) g(37)
f(18) i(58) s h(19).

A	D	E	F	G
86 − 29 = 57	98 − 19 = 79	47 − 18 = 29	46 − 28 = 18	55 − 18 = 37
H	**I**	**L**	**N**	**O**
88 − 69 = 19	94 − 36 = 58	37 − 28 = 9	60 − 38 = 22	85 − 37 = 48
R	**T**	**U**	**W**	**Y**
65 − 49 = 16	84 − 48 = 36	61 − 49 = 12	53 − 49 = 4	92 − 26 = 66

Page 27

Name ____________________ Skill: 2 digit from 2 digit, regrouping

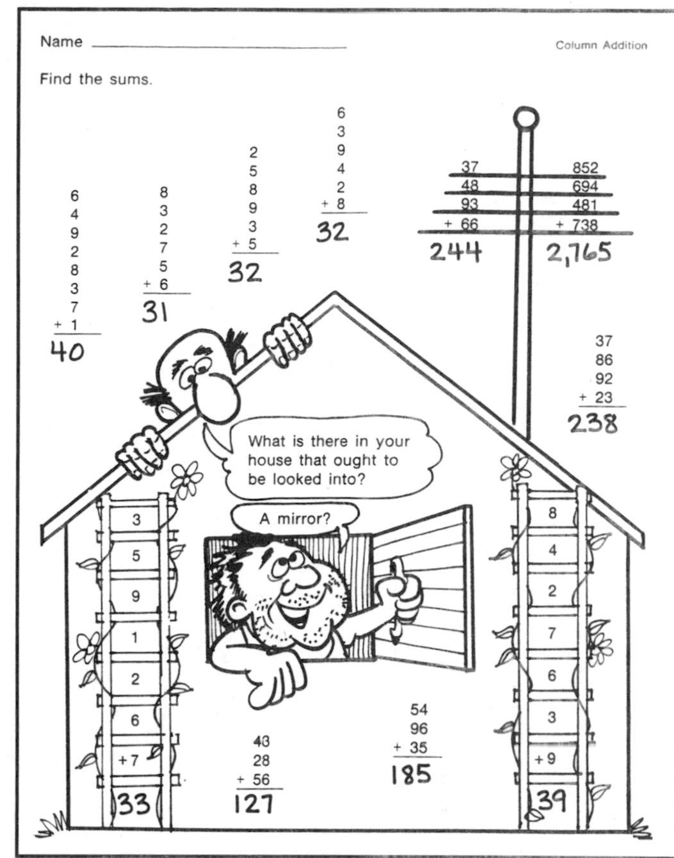

A Daffynition:

s(28) k(56) e(19) l(29) e(19) t(59) o(48) n(9) – a(37)
p(78) e(19) r(17) s(28) o(48) n(9) w(45) h(26) o(48) i(15) s(28)
i(15) n(9) s(28) i(15) d(6) e(19) o(48) u(7) t(59)

A	D	E	H	I
53 − 16 = 37	75 − 69 = 6	88 − 69 = 19	54 − 28 = 26	42 − 27 = 15
K	**L**	**N**	**O**	**P**
75 − 19 = 56	44 − 15 = 29	55 − 46 = 9	76 − 28 = 48	96 − 18 = 78
R	**S**	**T**	**U**	**W**
94 − 77 = 17	46 − 18 = 28	97 − 38 = 59	26 − 19 = 7	84 − 39 = 45

Page 28

Answer Key

Name ______________________ Skill: 2 digit from 2 digit, regrouping

A Riddle:

w h a t / i s / b l a c k
38 25 52 14 / 8 9 / 27 56 52 4 29

a n d / w h i t e / a n d
52 62 36 / 38 25 8 14 43 / 52 62 36

l i v e s / i n / t h e
56 8 77 43 9 / 8 62 / 14 25 43

d e s e r t?
36 43 9 43 6 14

A lost penguin.

A 81 − 29 = 52	**B** 46 − 19 = 27	**C** 53 − 49 = 4	**D** 65 − 29 = 36	**E** 82 − 39 = 43
H 44 − 19 = 25	**I** 97 − 89 = 8	**K** 45 − 16 = 29	**L** 85 − 29 = 56	**N** 81 − 19 = 62
R 25 − 19 = 6	**S** 77 − 68 = 9	**T** 53 − 39 = 14	**V** 95 − 18 = 77	**W** 86 − 48 = 38

Page 29

Name ______________________ Skill: 2 digit from 3 digit, regrouping

A Daffynition:

a u t o b i o g r a p h y –
724 159 511 237 812 914 237 558 428 724 345 777 103

t h e / s t o r y / o f
511 777 366 / 559 511 237 428 103 / 237 408

a / c a r
724 / 206 724 428

A 753 − 29 = 724	**B** 851 − 39 = 812	**C** 252 − 46 = 206	**E** 395 − 29 = 366	**F** 427 − 19 = 408
G 584 − 26 = 558	**H** 793 − 16 = 777	**I** 940 − 26 = 914	**O** 274 − 37 = 237	**P** 360 − 15 = 345
R 455 − 27 = 428	**S** 598 − 39 = 559	**T** 530 − 19 = 511	**U** 186 − 27 = 159	**Y** 190 − 87 = 103

Page 30

Name ______________________ Skill: 2 digit from 3 digit, regrouping

Riddle: Why do camels drink water?

T h e y / d o n ' t
769 604 816 158 / 537 918 445 769

k n o w / h o w / t o
735 445 918 247 / 604 918 247 / 769 918

o p e n / m i l k
918 326 816 445 / 506 913 132 735

b o t t l e s.
231 918 769 769 132 816 409

B 250 − 19 = 231	**D** 555 − 18 = 537	**E** 864 − 48 = 816	**H** 633 − 29 = 604	**I** 941 − 28 = 913
K 764 − 29 = 735	**L** 181 − 49 = 132	**M** 525 − 19 = 506	**N** 473 − 28 = 445	**O** 936 − 18 = 918
P 352 − 26 = 326	**S** 444 − 35 = 409	**T** 796 − 27 = 769	**W** 282 − 35 = 247	**Y** 193 − 35 = 158

Page 31

Name ______________________ Skill: 2 digit from 3 digit, regrouping

Riddle:

w h a t / i s / a
157 119 544 405 / 548 233 / 544

s c a r e d / s e a
233 718 544 446 316 909 / 233 316 544

m o n s t e r
931 936 233 405 316 446

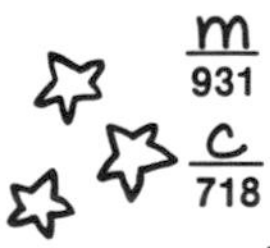

c a l l e d?
718 544 228 228 316 909

a / c h i c k e n / o f
544 / 718 119 548 718 349 316 936 / 657

t h e / s e a
405 119 316 / 233 316 544

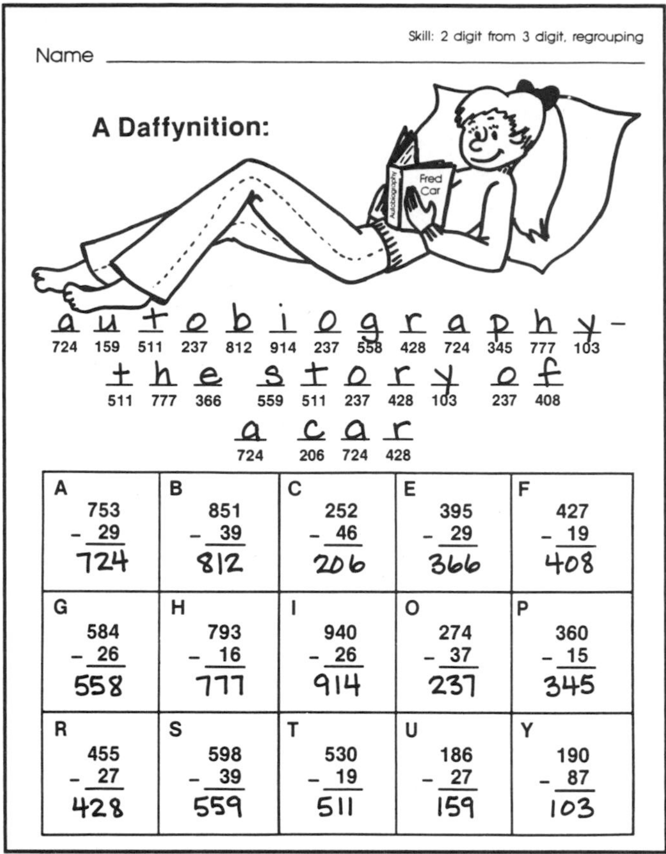

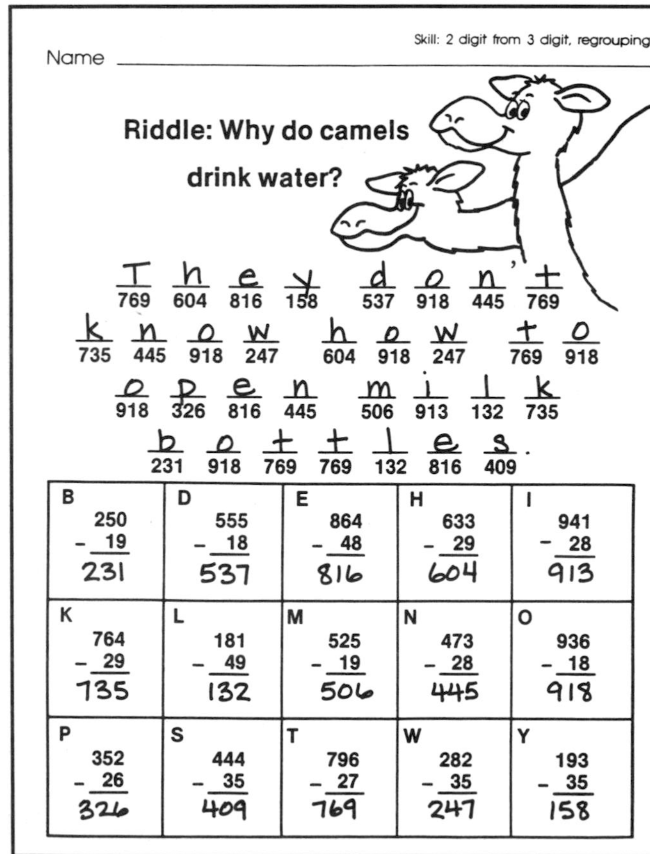

A 563 − 19 = 544	**C** 735 − 17 = 718	**D** 927 − 18 = 909	**E** 341 − 25 = 316	**F** 683 − 26 = 657
H 136 − 17 = 119	**I** 586 − 38 = 548	**K** 375 − 26 = 349	**L** 256 − 28 = 228	**M** 950 − 19 = 931
N 961 − 25 = 936	**R** 493 − 47 = 446	**S** 292 − 59 = 233	**T** 444 − 39 = 405	**W** 194 − 37 = 157

Page 32

Answer Key

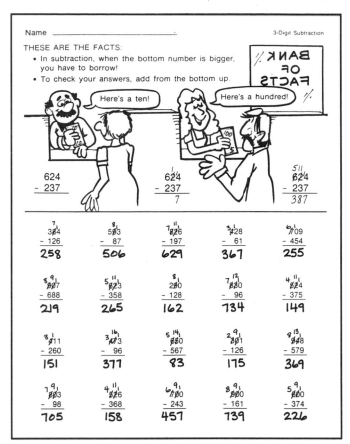

Name ______________________________ 3-Digit Subtraction

THESE ARE THE FACTS:

- In subtraction, when the bottom number is bigger, you have to borrow!
- To check your answers, add from the bottom up.

624 − 237	624 − 237 = 7	624 − 237 = 387

384 − 126 = 258	593 − 87 = 506	826 − 197 = 629	428 − 61 = 367	709 − 454 = 255
907 − 688 = 219	623 − 358 = 265	290 − 128 = 162	830 − 96 = 734	524 − 375 = 149
411 − 260 = 151	473 − 96 = 377	650 − 567 = 83	301 − 126 = 175	948 − 579 = 369
803 − 98 = 705	526 − 368 = 158	700 − 243 = 457	900 − 161 = 739	600 − 374 = 226

Page 33

Name ______________________________ 4-Digit Subtraction

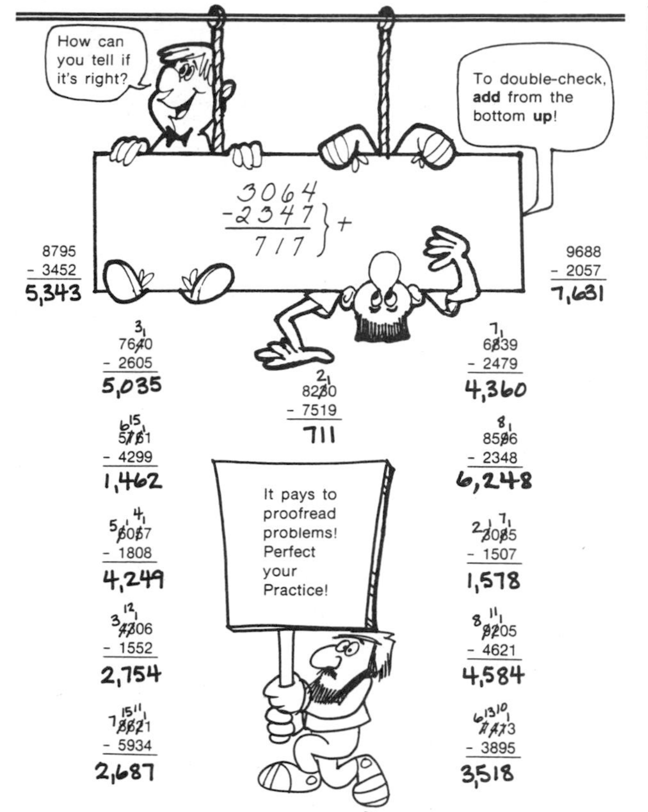

8795 − 3452 = 5,343		9688 − 2057 = 7,631
7640 − 2605 = 5,035	8230 − 7519 = 711	6839 − 2479 = 4,360
5761 − 4299 = 1,462		8596 − 2348 = 6,248
6057 − 1808 = 4,249		3085 − 1507 = 1,578
4306 − 1552 = 2,754		9205 − 4621 = 4,584
8621 − 5934 = 2,687		7413 − 3895 = 3,518

Page 34

Name ______________________________ Skill: Multiplying by 0, 1 and 2

Hop to It!

Write each product.

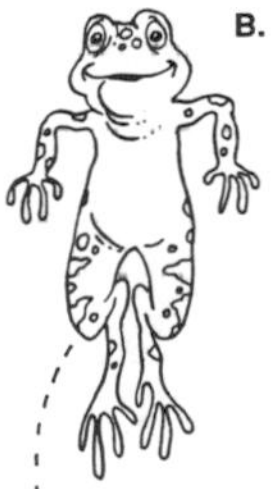

A.	B.	C.
0 x 0 = 0	7 x 1 = 7	4 x 2 = 8
8 x 0 = 0	1 x 1 = 1	9 x 2 = 18
2 x 0 = 0	5 x 1 = 5	3 x 2 = 6
7 x 0 = 0	6 x 1 = 6	0 x 2 = 0
4 x 0 = 0	3 x 1 = 3	8 x 2 = 16
5 x 0 = 0	8 x 1 = 8	2 x 2 = 4
9 x 0 = 0	0 x 1 = 0	6 x 2 = 12
1 x 0 = 0	4 x 1 = 4	1 x 2 = 2
6 x 0 = 0	2 x 1 = 2	5 x 2 = 10
3 x 0 = 0	9 x 1 = 9	7 x 2 = 14

Solve each problem.

D. 1 x 5 = 5	E. 2 x 1 = 2	F. 0 x 9 = 0	G. 2 x 4 = 8	H. 1 x 7 = 7	I. 2 x 8 = 16
J. 2 x 2 = 4	K. 1 x 0 = 0	L. 2 x 5 = 10	M. 1 x 3 = 3	N. 2 x 9 = 18	O. 1 x 2 = 2
P. 2 x 3 = 6	Q. 0 x 8 = 0	R. 2 x 7 = 14	S. 2 x 6 = 12		Score ___ / 46

Brainwork! If a number is multiplied by 2, the answer will always end in one of five numbers. Write the five numbers. (0, 2, 4, 6 or 8)

Page 35

Name ______________________________ Skill: multiplying by 1 and 2

A Riddle

What has thirty-six legs and goes to picnics?

a	h	u	n	g	r	y	a	n	t	f	a	m	i	l	y
6	8	12	18	2	10	16	6	18	14	3	6	5	7	9	16

A 3 X 2 = 6	F 3 X 1 = 3	G 1 X 2 = 2	H 4 X 2 = 8
I 7 X 1 = 7	L 9 X 1 = 9	M 5 X 1 = 5	N 9 X 2 = 18
R 5 X 2 = 10	T 7 X 2 = 14	U 6 X 2 = 12	Y 8 X 2 = 16

Page 36

Answer Key

Name ______________________ Skill: multiplying by 1 and 2

A Happy Thought

Share a chocolate malt with me.

10 16 6 12 4 / 6 / 18 16 9 18 9 8 6 7 4 / 14 6 8 7 / 3 2 7 16 / 14 4

A 3 X 2 = 6	C 9 X 2 = 18	E 2 X 2 = 4	H 8 X 2 = 16
I 1 X 2 = 2	L 4 X 2 = 8	M 7 X 2 = 14	O 9 X 1 = 9
R 6 X 2 = 12	S 5 X 2 = 10	T 7 X 1 = 7	W 3 X 1 = 3

Page 37

Name ______________________ Skill: multiplying by 1 and 2

A Tongue Twister

Beasties blow big blue bubbles.

0 6 10 9 12 2 6 9 / 0 5 1 7 / 0 2 4 / 0 5 3 6 / 0 3 0 0 5 6 9

A 5 X 2 = 10	B 0 X 1 = 0	E 6 X 1 = 6	F 7 X 2 = 14
G 4 X 1 = 4	I 2 X 1 = 2	L 5 X 1 = 5	O 1 X 1 = 1
S 9 X 1 = 9	T 6 X 2 = 12	U 3 X 1 = 3	W 7 X 1 = 7

Page 38

Name ______________________ Skill: multiplying by 2 and 3

A Riddle

What is white on the outside, green on the inside, and hops?

a frog sandwich

3 / 24 14 8 6 / 18 3 15 0 9 12 27 21

A 1 X 3 = 3	C 9 X 3 = 27	D 0 X 3 = 0	F 8 X 3 = 24
G 2 X 3 = 6	H 7 X 3 = 21	I 4 X 3 = 12	N 5 X 3 = 15
O 4 X 2 = 8	R 7 X 2 = 14	S 6 X 3 = 18	W 3 X 3 = 9

Page 39

Name ______________________ Skill: Multiplying by 3 and 4

Silly Seals

Write each product. Cross off the answer on the matching ball.

A.
5 x 3 = 15
1 x 3 = 3
6 x 3 = 18
3 x 3 = 9
9 x 3 = 27
0 x 3 = 0
4 x 3 = 12
2 x 3 = 6
8 x 3 = 24
7 x 3 = 21

B.
9 x 4 = 36
3 x 4 = 12
8 x 4 = 32
7 x 4 = 28
0 x 4 = 0
4 x 4 = 16
6 x 4 = 24
1 x 4 = 4
5 x 4 = 20
2 x 4 = 8

Solve each problem.

C. 3 x 8 = 24	D. 4 x 1 = 4	E. 3 x 9 = 27	F. 4 x 4 = 16	G. 3 x 5 = 15	H. 4 x 8 = 32
I. 3 x 6 = 18	J. 3 x 0 = 0	K. 4 x 5 = 20	L. 3 x 3 = 9	M. 4 x 9 = 36	N. 3 x 2 = 6
O. 4 x 3 = 12	P. 3 x 7 = 21	Q. 4 x 7 = 28	R. 4 x 6 = 24		Score ___ / 36

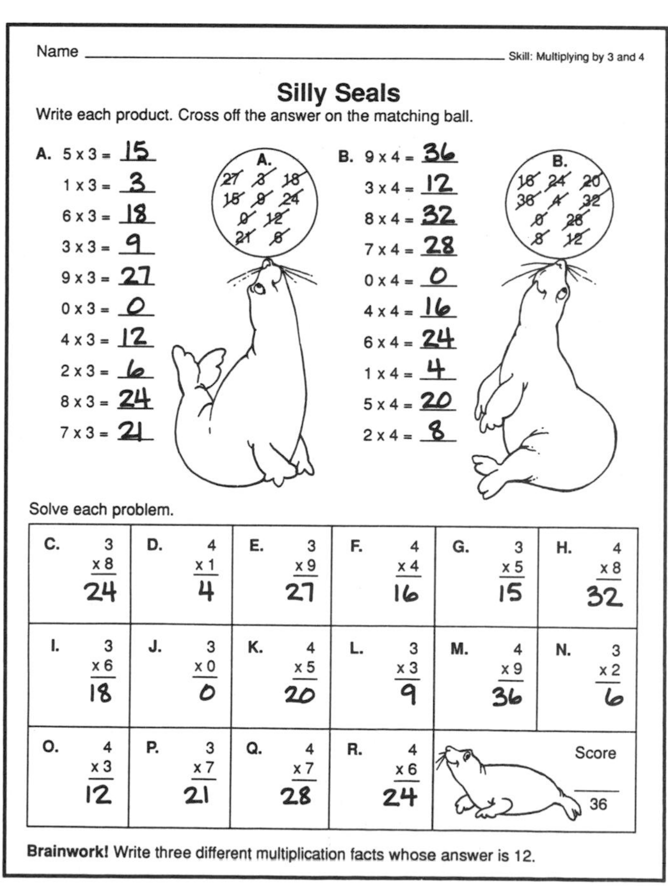

Brainwork! Write three different multiplication facts whose answer is 12.

Page 40

Answer Key

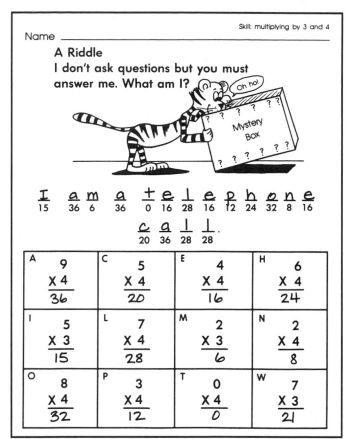

Name ____________________ Skill: multiplying by 3 and 4

A Riddle
I don't ask questions but you must answer me. What am I?

I am a telephone call.
15 36 6 36 0 16 28 16 12 24 32 8 16
20 36 28 28

A: 9 X 4 = 36	C: 5 X 4 = 20	E: 4 X 4 = 16	H: 6 X 4 = 24
I: 5 X 3 = 15	L: 7 X 4 = 28	M: 2 X 3 = 6	N: 2 X 4 = 8
O: 8 X 4 = 32	P: 3 X 4 = 12	T: 0 X 4 = 0	W: 7 X 3 = 21

Page 41

Name ____________________ Skill: multiplying by 2, 3 and 4

A Riddle
What pine has the sharpest needles?

an angry porcupine
6 28 6 28 15 24 16
18 33 24 20 0 18 36 28 2

A: 3 X 2 = 6	C: 5 X 4 = 20	E: 1 X 2 = 2	G: 5 X 3 = 15
I: 9 X 4 = 36	N: 7 X 4 = 28	O: 11 X 3 = 33	P: 9 X 2 = 18
R: 8 X 3 = 24	U: 0 X 3 = 0	Y: 4 X 4 = 16	Z: 9 X 3 = 27

Page 42

Name ____________________ Skill: multiplying by 5

Daffynition: Snowbank:

a polar bear money bank
20 30 35 0 20 10 5 50 20 10
55 35 40 50 15 5 20 40 25

A: 4 X 5 = 20	B: 1 X 5 = 5	E: 10 X 5 = 50	K: 5 X 5 = 25
L: 0 X 5 = 0	M: 11 X 5 = 55	N: 8 X 5 = 40	O: 7 X 5 = 35
P: 6 X 5 = 30	R: 2 X 5 = 10	Y: 3 X 5 = 15	Z: 9 X 5 = 45

Page 43

Name ____________________ Skill: multiplying by 4 and 5

A Tongue Twister

Five frogs with flat feet fell far.
24 4 16 36 24 0 44 40 5 4 8 15
24 20 12 8 24 36 36 8 24 36 20 20
24 12 0

A: 3 X 4 = 12	E: 9 X 4 = 36	F: 6 X 4 = 24	G: 10 X 4 = 40
H: 3 X 5 = 15	I: 1 X 4 = 4	L: 4 X 5 = 20	O: 11 X 4 = 44
R: 0 X 4 = 0	T: 2 X 4 = 8	V: 4 X 4 = 16	W: 1 X 5 = 5

Page 44

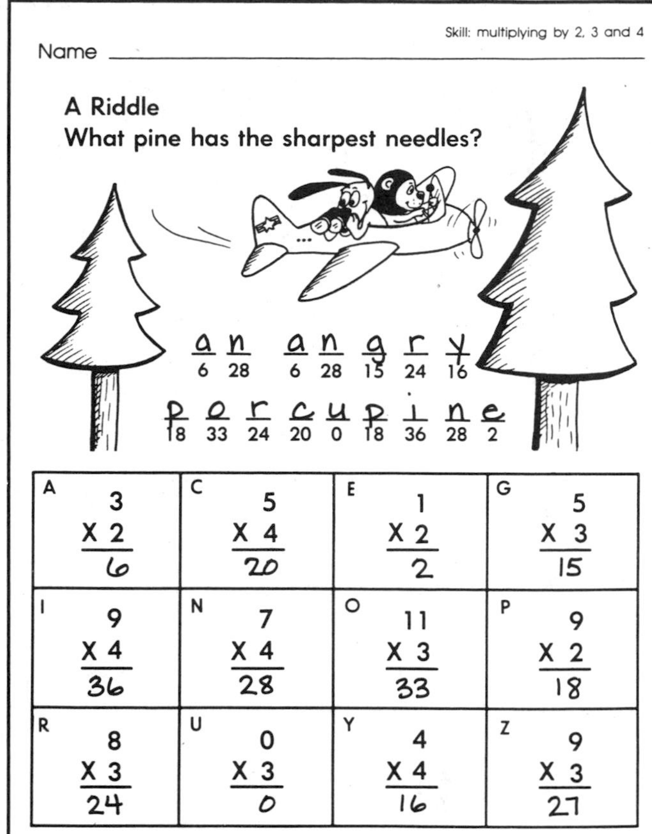

Answer Key

Skill: multiplying by 3, 4 and 5

Name ____________________

O p e n t h e b o t t l e - (8 32 15 16 45 10 15 25 8 45 45 27 15)

p o u r h i m o u t ! (32 8 40 21 10 24 9 8 40 45)

B: 5 x 5 = 25	E: 3 x 5 = 15	H: 2 x 5 = 10	I: 6 x 4 = 24
L: 9 x 3 = 27	M: 3 x 3 = 9	N: 4 x 4 = 16	O: 2 x 4 = 8
P: 8 x 4 = 32	R: 7 x 3 = 21	T: 9 x 5 = 45	U: 10 x 4 = 40

Page 45

Skill: multiplying by 6

Name ____________________

A Riddle

Why did the rocket lose its job?

I t w a s f i r e d (24 42 18 12 54 36 24 6 48 30)

M o n d a y. (72 60 0 30 12)

A: 2 X 6 = 12	D: 5 X 6 = 30	E: 8 X 6 = 48	F: 6 X 6 = 36
I: 4 X 6 = 24	M: 12 X 6 = 72	N: 0 X 6 = 0	O: 10 X 6 = 60
R: 1 X 6 = 6	S: 9 X 6 = 54	T: 7 X 6 = 42	W: 3 X 6 = 18

Page 46

Skill: multiplying by 6

Name ____________________

A Happy Thought

I s n ' t i t g r e a t (0 18 30 48 0 48 42 6 12 54 48)

t o b e d i f f e r e n t ! (48 60 66 12 24 0 36 36 12 6 12 30 48)

A: 9 X 6 = 54	B: 11 X 6 = 66	D: 4 X 6 = 24	E: 2 X 6 = 12
F: 6 X 6 = 36	G: 7 X 6 = 42	I: 0 X 6 = 0	N: 5 X 6 = 30
O: 10 X 6 = 60	R: 1 X 6 = 6	S: 3 X 6 = 18	T: 8 X 6 = 48

Page 47

Name ____________________ Skill: Multiplying by 5 and 6

Know-It-All Knights

Write each product. Cross off the answer on the matching shield.

A. 4 x 5 = 20
3 x 5 = 15
8 x 5 = 40
7 x 5 = 35
0 x 5 = 0
9 x 5 = 45
5 x 5 = 25
1 x 5 = 5
6 x 5 = 30
2 x 5 = 10

B. 3 x 6 = 18
1 x 6 = 6
6 x 6 = 36
5 x 6 = 30
9 x 6 = 54
0 x 6 = 0
7 x 6 = 42
2 x 6 = 12
8 x 6 = 48
4 x 6 = 24

Solve each problem.

C. 6 x 7 = 42	D. 5 x 8 = 40	E. 5 x 3 = 15	F. 6 x 4 = 24	G. 5 x 7 = 35	H. 6 x 5 = 30
I. 6 x 6 = 36	J. 6 x 0 = 0	K. 5 x 5 = 25	L. 6 x 9 = 54	M. 5 x 9 = 45	N. 5 x 1 = 5
O. 5 x 4 = 20	P. 6 x 8 = 48	Q. 5 x 7 = 35	R. 6 x 2 = 12		Score ____ 36

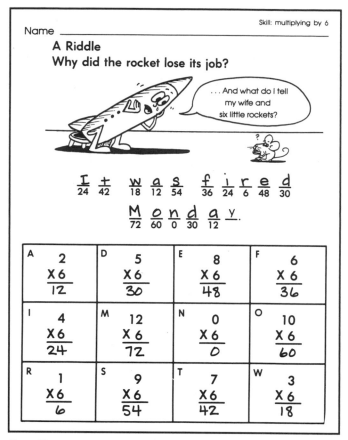

Brainwork! If a number is multiplied by 5, the answer will always end in one of two numbers. Write the two numbers. (0 or 5)

Page 48

Answer Key

Skill: multiplying by 7

Name ______________________________

A Tongue Twister

If you want to catch big trout, you need the right bait . . .

G r o w (7 70 21 84) g i a n t (7 49 14 28 63) g r e e n (7 70 56 56 28)

g r a s s h o p p e r s. (7 70 14 77 77 35 21 0 0 56 70 77)

A: 2 X 7 = 14	E: 8 X 7 = 56	G: 1 X 7 = 7	H: 5 X 7 = 35
I: 7 X 7 = 49	N: 4 X 7 = 28	O: 3 X 7 = 21	P: 0 X 7 = 0
R: 10 X 7 = 70	S: 11 X 7 = 77	T: 9 X 7 = 63	W: 12 X 7 = 84

Page 49

Skill: multiplying by 6 and 7

Name ______________________________

A Riddle
What do spooks eat for breakfast?

slurp
munch

g h o s t (7 63 14 24 21) t o a s t i e s (21 14 56 24 21 18 0 24)

a n d (56 30 35) m i l k (18 12 49)

A: 8 X 7 = 56	D: 5 X 7 = 35	E: 0 X 7 = 0	G: 1 X 7 = 7
H: 9 X 7 = 63	I: 3 X 6 = 18	K: 7 X 7 = 49	L: 2 X 6 = 12
N: 5 X 6 = 30	O: 2 X 7 = 14	S: 4 X 6 = 24	T: 3 X 7 = 21

Page 50

Skill: multiplying by 7

Name ______________________________

A Riddle
If cows have horns.....

W h y (56 63 14) d o n't (28 35 42 77) t h e y (77 63 0 14)

g o (21 35) b e e p - b e e p? (7 0 0 49 - 7 0 0 49)

B: 1 X 7 = 7	D: 4 X 7 = 28	E: 0 X 7 = 0	G: 3 X 7 = 21
H: 9 X 7 = 63	N: 6 X 7 = 42	O: 5 X 7 = 35	P: 7 X 7 = 49
T: 11 X 7 = 77	W: 8 X 7 = 56	Y: 2 X 7 = 14	Z: 10 X 7 = 70

Page 51

Skill: multiplying by 5, 6 and 7

Name ______________________________

Daffynition:

a s t r o n o m e r - (35 49 14 30 54 15 54 25 5 30)

a (35) n i g h t (15 24 42 21 14) w a t c h m a n (35 14 48 21 25 35 15)

A: 5 X 7 = 35	C: 8 X 6 = 48	E: 1 X 5 = 5	G: 6 X 7 = 42
H: 3 X 7 = 21	I: 4 X 6 = 24	M: 5 X 5 = 25	N: 3 X 5 = 15
O: 9 X 6 = 54	R: 5 X 6 = 30	S: 7 X 7 = 49	T: 2 X 7 = 14

Page 52

Answer Key

Name ______________________ Skill: Multiplying by 7 and 8

Skydiving

Write each product. Cross off the answer on the matching parachute.

A. 4 x 7 = 28
7 x 7 = 49
1 x 7 = 7
3 x 7 = 21
5 x 7 = 35
6 x 7 = 42
0 x 7 = 0
2 x 7 = 14
9 x 7 = 63
8 x 7 = 56

B. 8 x 8 = 64
3 x 8 = 24
0 x 8 = 0
7 x 8 = 56
4 x 8 = 32
1 x 8 = 8
6 x 8 = 48
9 x 8 = 72
2 x 8 = 16
5 x 8 = 40

Solve each problem.

C. 8 x 6 = 48	D. 7 x 1 = 7	E. 7 x 5 = 35	F. 8 x 4 = 32	G. 7 x 7 = 49	H. 8 x 8 = 64
I. 8 x 5 = 40	J. 8 x 0 = 0	K. 7 x 9 = 63	L. 8 x 3 = 24	M. 8 x 9 = 72	N. 7 x 2 = 14
O. 7 x 3 = 21	P. 7 x 8 = 56	Q. 8 x 2 = 16	R. 7 x 6 = 42		Score ___ 36

Brainwork! Write a word problem that can be solved using this fact: 7 x 8 = 56

Page 53

Name ______________________ Skill: multiplying by 8

A Riddle

What can you do if your pet monster hurts his toe?

You can call a tow (toe) truck.

Y o u c a n c a l l — 80 0 8 24 72 88 24 72 16 16

a t o w (t o e) t r u c k. — 72 40 0 32 (40 0 48) 40 56 8 24 64

A 9 X 8 = 72	C 3 X 8 = 24	E 6 X 8 = 48	K 8 X 8 = 64
L 2 X 8 = 16	N 11 X 8 = 88	O 0 X 8 = 0	R 7 X 8 = 56
T 5 X 8 = 40	U 1 X 8 = 8	W 4 X 8 = 32	Y 10 X 8 = 80

Page 54

Name ______________________ Skill: multiplying by 9

A Riddle

Daffynition: Caterpillar

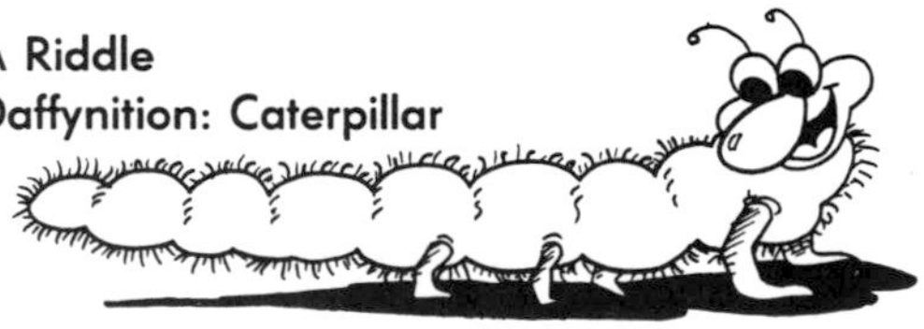

a worm in a big sweater

a w o r m i n a b i g — 72 54 90 36 27 81 63 72 9 81 99

s w e a t e r — 18 54 45 72 0 45 36

A 8 X 9 = 72	B 1 X 9 = 9	E 5 X 9 = 45	G 11 X 9 = 99
I 9 X 9 = 81	M 3 X 9 = 27	N 7 X 9 = 63	O 10 X 9 = 90
R 4 X 9 = 36	S 2 X 9 = 18	T 0 X 9 = 0	W 6 X 9 = 54

Page 55

Name ______________________ Skill: multiplying by 8 and 9

A Tongue Twister

Fourteen fearless fireflies flew fast.

F o u r t e e n — 45 16 54 0 40 18 18 48

f e a r l e s s — 45 18 56 0 9 18 36 36

f i r e f l i e s f l e w — 45 32 0 18 45 9 32 18 36 45 9 18 24

f a s t. — 45 56 36 40

A 8 X 7 = 56	E 2 X 9 = 18	F 5 X 9 = 45	I 4 X 8 = 32
L 1 X 9 = 9	N 6 X 8 = 48	O 2 X 8 = 16	R 0 X 8 = 0
S 4 X 9 = 36	T 5 X 8 = 40	U 6 X 9 = 54	W 3 X 8 = 24

Page 56

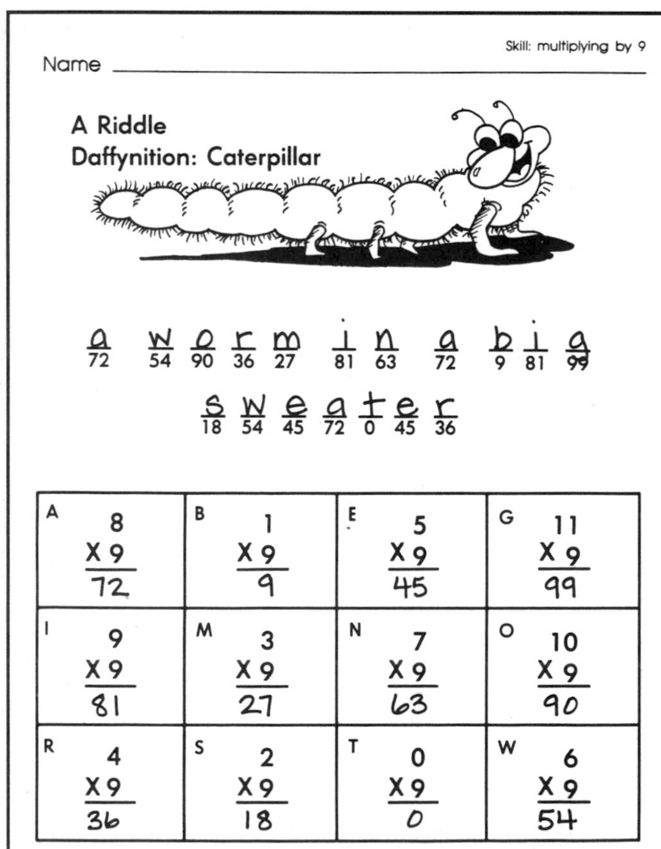

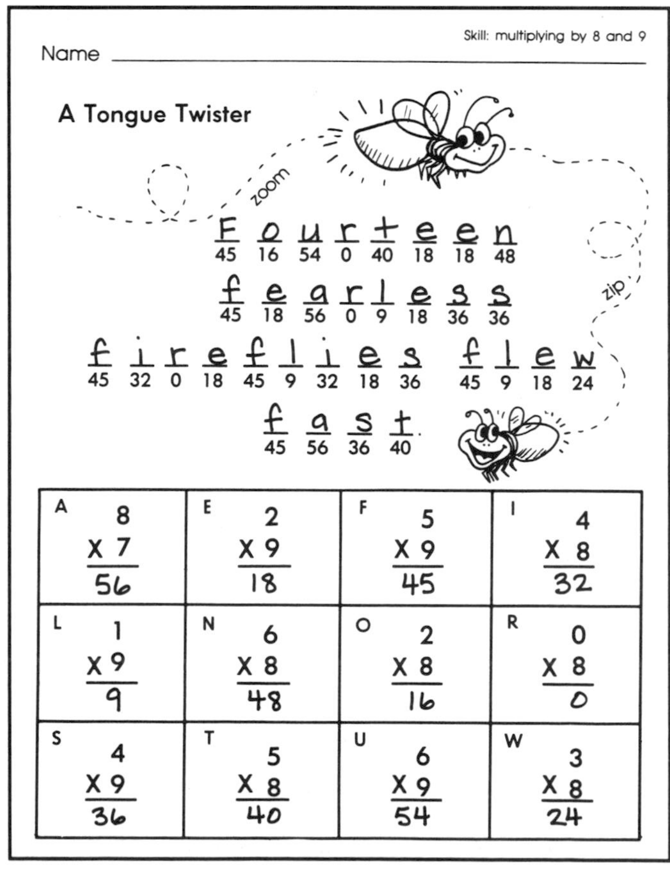

Answer Key

Page 57

Name ______________________ Skill: Multiplying by 9 and 10

A Bright Bouquet

Write each product. Cross off the answer on the matching flowers.

A.
2 x 9 = 18
9 x 9 = 81
0 x 9 = 0
3 x 9 = 27
4 x 9 = 36
10 x 9 = 90
7 x 9 = 63
1 x 9 = 9
5 x 9 = 45
8 x 9 = 72
6 x 9 = 54

B.
5 x 10 = 50
3 x 10 = 30
10 x 10 = 100
7 x 10 = 70
0 x 10 = 0
2 x 10 = 20
6 x 10 = 60
1 x 10 = 10
8 x 10 = 80
9 x 10 = 90
4 x 10 = 40

Solve each problem.

C. 9 x 9 = 81	D. 10 x 0 = 0	E. 9 x 3 = 27	F. 10 x 4 = 40	G. 9 x 8 = 72	H. 10 x 6 = 60
I. 9 x 6 = 54	J. 9 x 1 = 9	K. 10 x 5 = 50	L. 9 x 7 = 63	M. 10 x 9 = 90	N. 10 x 10 = 100
O. 10 x 3 = 30	P. 9 x 2 = 18	Q. 9 x 4 = 36	R. 10 x 8 = 80		Score ___ 38

Brainwork! Look at your answers for problems with 9 as a factor. If you add the digits in each answer, what number will you always get? (9-unless answer is 0)

Page 57

Page 58

Name ______________________ Skill: multiplying by 9 and 10

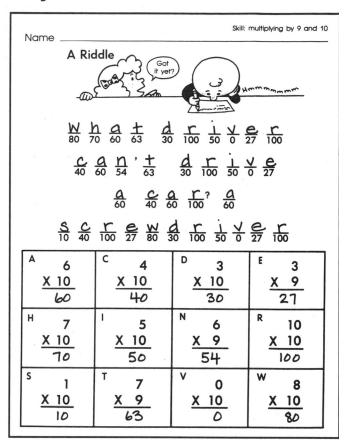

A Riddle

w h a t   d r i v e r
80 70 60 63   30 100 50 0 27 100

c a n ' t   d r i v e
40 60 54 63   30 100 50 0 27

a   c a r ?   a
60   40 60 100   60

s c r e w d r i v e r
10 40 100 27 80 30 100 50 0 27 100

A 6 X 10 = 60	C 4 X 10 = 40	D 3 X 10 = 30	E 3 X 9 = 27
H 7 X 10 = 70	I 5 X 10 = 50	N 6 X 9 = 54	R 10 X 10 = 100
S 1 X 10 = 10	T 7 X 9 = 63	V 0 X 10 = 0	W 8 X 10 = 80

Page 58

Page 59

Name ______________________ Skill: Multiplying by 11 and 12

Dinosaur Duo

Write each product. Cross off the answer on the matching dinosaur.

A.
6 x 11 = 66
4 x 11 = 44
3 x 11 = 33
10 x 11 = 110
7 x 11 = 77
0 x 11 = 0
11 x 11 = 121
1 x 11 = 11
9 x 11 = 99
12 x 11 = 132
5 x 11 = 55
2 x 11 = 22
8 x 11 = 88

B.
5 x 12 = 60
3 x 12 = 36
10 x 12 = 120
8 x 12 = 96
6 x 12 = 72
12 x 12 = 144
4 x 12 = 48
0 x 12 = 0
7 x 12 = 84
9 x 12 = 108
11 x 12 = 132
1 x 12 = 12
2 x 12 = 24

Solve each problem.

C. 12 x 3 = 36	D. 11 x 5 = 55	E. 12 x 12 = 144	F. 11 x 4 = 44	G. 12 x 6 = 72	H. 11 x 9 = 99
I. 12 x 2 = 24	J. 12 x 1 = 12	K. 11 x 11 = 121	L. 12 x 4 = 48	M. 11 x 0 = 0	N. 11 x 10 = 110
O. 11 x 7 = 77	P. 12 x 5 = 60	Q. 12 x 9 = 108	R. 11 x 8 = 88		Score ___ 42

Brainwork! Write a multiplication word problem that uses the word *dozen.*

Page 59

Page 60

Name ______________________ Skill: Multiplying by multiples of 10

Terrific Tens

Multiply.

A. 6 x 1 = 6
6 x 10 = 60

B. 3 x 4 = 12
3 x 40 = 120

C. 5 x 7 = 35
5 x 70 = 350

D. 8 x 2 = 16
8 x 20 = 160

E. 6 x 6 = 36
6 x 60 = 360

F. 9 x 6 = 54
9 x 60 = 540

G. 4 x 7 = 28
40 x 7 = 280

H. 8 x 5 = 40
8 x 50 = 400

I. 9 x 3 = 27
90 x 3 = 270

J. 7 x 3 = 21
7 x 30 = 210

K. 5 x 5 = 25
50 x 5 = 250

L. 7 x 0 = 0
70 x 0 = 0

M. 4 x 8 = 32
4 x 80 = 320

N. 3 x 6 = 18
30 x 6 = 180

O. 8 x 8 = 64
80 x 8 = 640

Solve each problem.

P. 20 x 9 = 180	Q. 20 x 3 = 60	R. 30 x 5 = 150	S. 40 x 4 = 160	T. 50 x 2 = 100	U. 90 x 9 = 810
V. 80 x 9 = 720	W. 70 x 7 = 490	X. 40 x 0 = 0	Y. 10 x 8 = 80		Score ___ 40

Brainwork! Use these numbers (3, 4, 6, 8, 30, 40, 60, 80) to write four multiplication problems whose answer is 240.

Page 60

Answer Key

Road Rally

Name ______________________ Skill: Multiplying 2-digit by 1-digit numbers

Solve each problem by multiplying. Cross off the answer on the car.

A. 24 x 2 = 48
B. 86 x 1 = 86
C. 13 x 3 = 39
D. 20 x 4 = 80
E. 97 x 0 = 0
F. 14 x 2 = 28
G. 71 x 6 = 426
H. 63 x 3 = 189
I. 52 x 4 = 208
J. 91 x 5 = 455
K. 40 x 6 = 240
L. 82 x 3 = 246
M. 19 x 1 = 19
N. 22 x 2 = 44
O. 31 x 4 = 124
P. 60 x 7 = 420
Q. 41 x 8 = 328
R. 33 x 3 = 99
S. 92 x 4 = 368
T. 71 x 4 = 284
U. 52 x 3 = 156
V. 81 x 7 = 567
W. 72 x 3 = 216
X. 61 x 9 = 549
Y. 50 x 5 = 250

Brainwork! If a car traveled the 52-mile Road Rally route four times, how many miles did it travel altogether? (208 miles)

Page 61

Multiplication: 2 Digits × 1 Digit

Name ______________________

Find the products.

23 × 3 = 69
37 × 4 = 148
95 × 2 = 190

38 × 2 = 76
86 × 5 = 430
27 × 3 = 81
49 × 2 = 98
65 × 4 = 260
18 × 5 = 90

46 × 3 = 138
20 × 4 = 80
49 × 2 = 98
52 × 7 = 364
93 × 8 = 744
72 × 6 = 432

19 × 7 = 133
38 × 8 = 304
64 × 6 = 384
42 × 9 = 378
80 × 5 = 400
24 × 7 = 168

48 × 7 = 336
15 × 9 = 135
36 × 8 = 288
57 × 7 = 399
19 × 9 = 171
60 × 7 = 420

Page 62

Fanciful Flight

Name ______________________ Skill: Multiplying 2-digit by 1-digit numbers, Regrouping

Solve each problem by multiplying.
Cross off the answer on the butterfly.

Score ____ 25

67 x 5 = 335

A. 19 x 2 = 38
B. 34 x 8 = 272
C. 63 x 9 = 567
D. 15 x 8 = 120
E. 49 x 5 = 245
F. 53 x 6 = 318
G. 27 x 4 = 108
H. 37 x 3 = 111
I. 28 x 7 = 196
J. 48 x 9 = 432
K. 65 x 3 = 195
L. 17 x 7 = 119
M. 88 x 2 = 176
N. 61 x 6 = 366
O. 86 x 8 = 688
P. 24 x 4 = 96
Q. 55 x 5 = 275
R. 31 x 9 = 279
S. 56 x 7 = 392

T. 36 x 3 = 108
U. 42 x 6 = 252
V. 93 x 4 = 372
W. 85 x 2 = 170
X. 39 x 7 = 273
Y. 19 x 8 = 152

Brainwork! If Dawn saw 13 butterflies and each had 6 spots on its wings, how many butterfly spots did she see? (78 spots)

Page 63

Toy Store

Name ______________________ Skill: Multiplying money by 1-digit numbers, Regrouping

Score ____ 20

Solve each problem by multiplying. Cross off the answer on the list of receipts.

$1.75 x 6 = $10.50

A. $.71 x 8 = $5.68
B. $.25 x 4 = $1.00
C. $.36 x 5 = $1.80
D. $.42 x 3 = $1.26
E. $1.50 x 8 = $12.00
F. $6.00 x 6 = $36.00
G. $3.19 x 5 = $15.95
H. $5.82 x 6 = $34.92
I. $1.25 x 9 = $11.25
J. $8.09 x 9 = $72.81
K. $.57 x 7 = $3.99
L. $3.99 x 2 = $7.98
M. $6.17 x 4 = $24.68
N. $1.09 x 7 = $7.63
O. $7.08 x 3 = $21.24
P. $4.36 x 9 = $39.24
Q. $9.72 x 7 = $68.04
R. $5.82 x 2 = $11.64
S. $8.04 x 8 = $64.32
T. $4.60 x 4 = $18.40

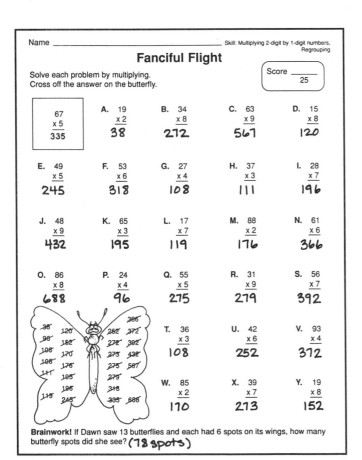

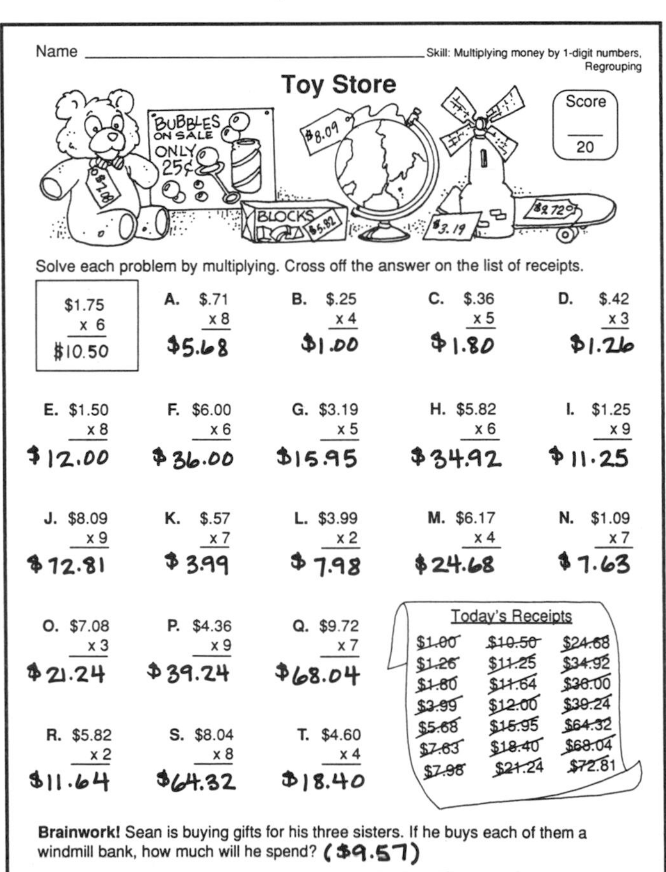

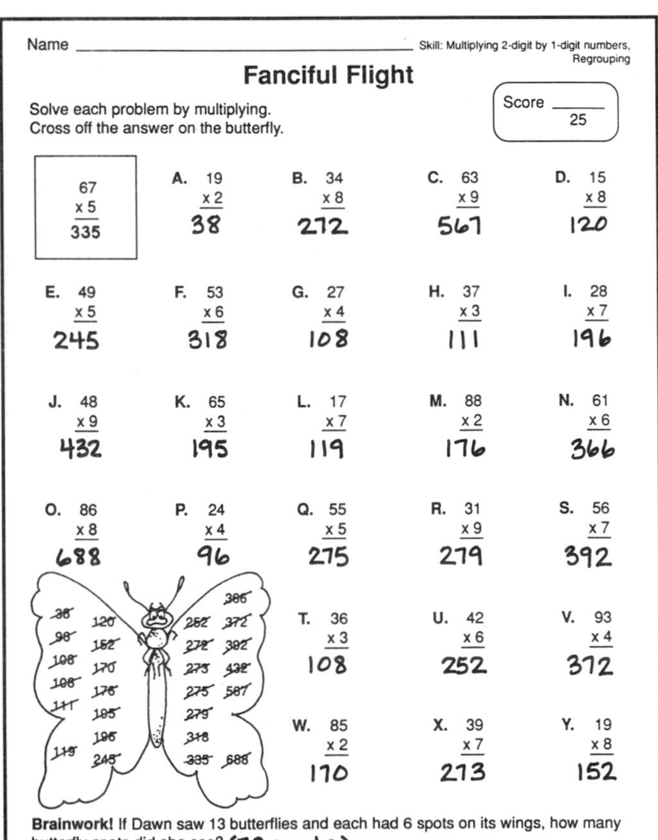

Brainwork! Sean is buying gifts for his three sisters. If he buys each of them a windmill bank, how much will he spend? ($9.57)

Page 64

Answer Key

Name ______________________ Skill: Multiplying by multiples of 100

Happy Hundreds

Multiply.

A. 4 x 1 = 4
4 x 10 = 40
4 x 100 = 400

D. 5 x 6 = 30
50 x 6 = 300
500 x 6 = 3,000

G. 8 x 8 = 64
80 x 8 = 640
800 x 8 = 6,400

B. 7 x 3 = 21
7 x 30 = 210
7 x 300 = 2,100

E. 8 x 7 = 56
8 x 70 = 560
800 x 7 = 5,600

H. 4 x 5 = 20
4 x 50 = 200
4 x 500 = 2,000

C. 9 x 9 = 81
9 x 90 = 810
9 x 900 = 8,100

F. 6 x 2 = 12
60 x 2 = 120
6 x 200 = 1,200

Solve each problem.

I. 800 x 6 = 4,800	J. 900 x 4 = 3,600	K. 500 x 5 = 2,500	L. 300 x 8 = 2,400	M. 700 x 2 = 1,400	N. 400 x 6 = 2,400
O. 200 x 2 = 400	P. 400 x 8 = 3,200	Q. 600 x 7 = 4,200	R. 900 x 0 = 0	S. 300 x 6 = 1,800	T. 400 x 2 = 800
U. 100 x 7 = 700	V. 200 x 5 = 1,000	W. 600 x 9 = 5,400	X. 300 x 3 = 900		Score ___ 40

Brainwork! Study the pattern above. Then solve these problems.
7 x 3,000 = 21,000   9,000 x 8 = 72,000   2 x 60,000 = 120,000

Page 65

Name ______________________ Skill: Multiplying 3-digit by 1-digit numbers, Regrouping

Penguin Power

Solve each problem by multiplying.
Cross off the answer on the ice hole.

Score ___ 25

126 x 3 = 378	A. 374 x 2 = 748	B. 151 x 9 = 1,359	C. 304 x 7 = 2,128	D. 519 x 4 = 2,076
	E. 916 x 5 = 4,580	F. 573 x 6 = 3,438	G. 218 x 4 = 872	H. 835 x 8 = 6,680	I. 708 x 9 = 6,372
	J. 709 x 7 = 4,963	K. 324 x 5 = 1,620	L. 783 x 3 = 2,349	M. 196 x 8 = 1,568	N. 186 x 6 = 1,116
	O. 920 x 9 = 8,280	P. 934 x 4 = 3,736	Q. 492 x 6 = 2,952	R. 182 x 2 = 364	S. 582 x 7 = 4,074
			T. 307 x 8 = 2,456	U. 550 x 6 = 3,300	V. 954 x 3 = 2,862
			W. 875 x 5 = 4,375	X. 223 x 9 = 2,007	Y. 609 x 2 = 1,218

Brainwork! If 329 penguins were each flapping their two flippers, how many penguin flippers would be flapping? (658 flippers)

Page 66

Name ______________________ Multiplication: 3 Digits × 1 Digit

Find the products.

415 × 3 = 1,245	987 × 2 = 1,974	328 × 5 = 1,640	238 × 4 = 952	156 × 3 = 468
864 × 5 = 4,320	276 × 4 = 1,104	529 × 3 = 1,587	190 × 2 = 380	209 × 4 = 836
748 × 5 = 3,740	486 × 3 = 1,458	507 × 4 = 2,028	359 × 5 = 1,795	908 × 2 = 1,816
550 × 7 = 3,850	517 × 6 = 3,102	128 × 9 = 1,152	463 × 8 = 3,704	418 × 7 = 2,926
944 × 9 = 8,496	308 × 7 = 2,156	291 × 8 = 2,328	674 × 6 = 4,044	890 × 9 = 8,010
327 × 8 = 2,616	876 × 9 = 7,884	909 × 6 = 5,454	463 × 7 = 3,241	608 × 8 = 4,864

Page 67

Name ______________________ Skill: Multiplying 2-digit by 2-digit numbers, Regrouping

There She Blows!

Solve by multiplying. Cross off the answer on the whale.

Score ___ 15

67 x 32 = 134 + 2010 = 2,144	A. 31 x 23 = 93 + 620 = 713	B. 90 x 58 = 720 + 4500 = 5,220	C. 53 x 20 = 00 + 1060 = 1,060
D. 71 x 46 = 426 + 2840 = 3,266	E. 52 x 44 = 208 + 2080 = 2,288	F. 82 x 64 = 328 + 4920 = 5,248	G. 68 x 70 = 00 + 4760 = 4,760
H. 94 x 42 = 188 + 3760 = 3,948	I. 73 x 25 = 365 + 1460 = 1,825	J. 59 x 66 = 354 + 3540 = 3,894	K. 25 x 18 = 200 + 250 = 450
L. 41 x 96 = 246 + 3690 = 3,936	M. 78 x 65 = 390 + 4680 = 5,070	N. 18 x 78 = 144 + 1260 = 1,404	O. 99 x 99 = 891 + 8910 = 9,801

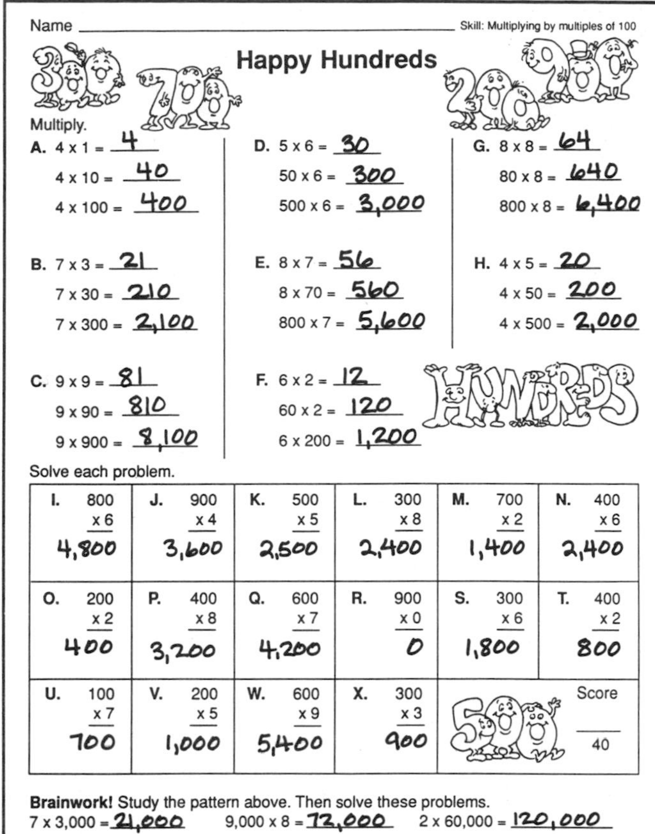

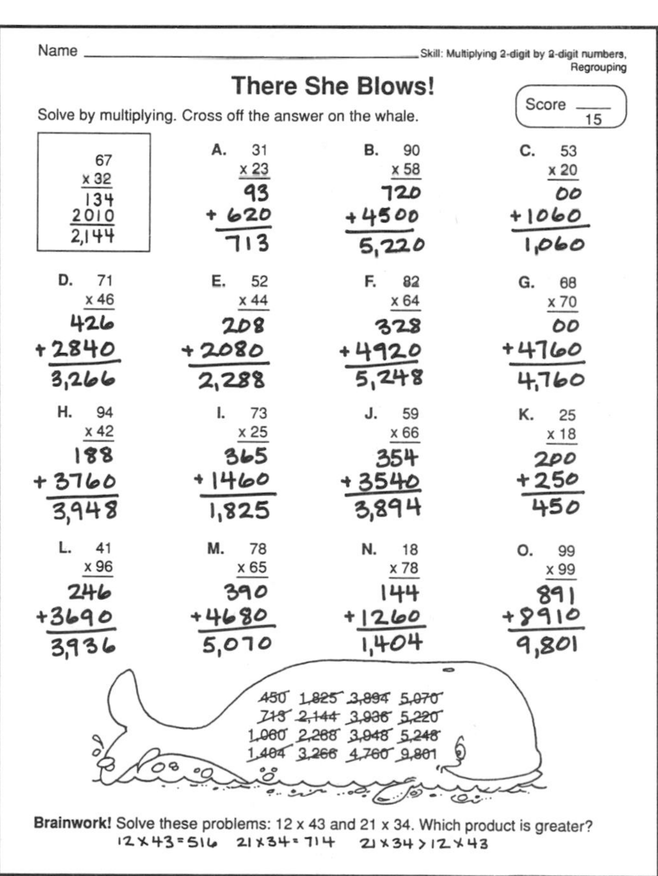

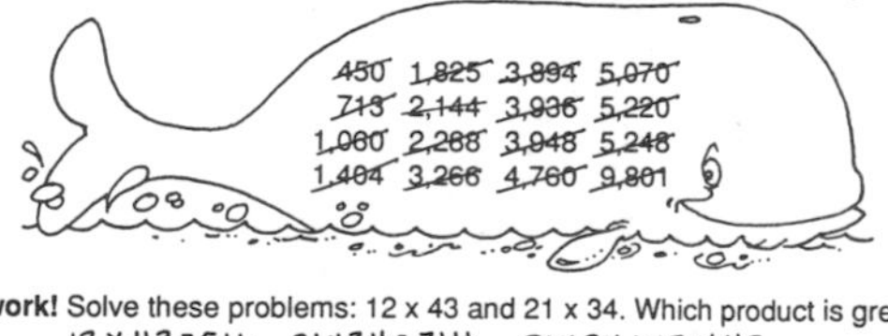

Brainwork! Solve these problems: 12 x 43 and 21 x 34. Which product is greater?
12 x 43 = 516   21 x 34 = 714   21 x 34 > 12 x 43

Page 68

Answer Key

Name ______________________ Multiplication: 2 Digits × 2 Digits

Multiply. Then add the products.

25 × 48 200 +1000 1,200	47 × 56 282 +2350 2,632	83 × 34 332 +2490 2,822	36 × 92 72 +3240 3,312	
42 × 49 378 +1680 2,058	50 × 87 350 +4000 4,350	71 × 58 568 +3550 4,118	63 × 79 567 +4410 4,977	38 × 29 342 +760 1,102
56 × 33 168 +1680 1,848	84 × 25 420 +1680 2,100	27 × 54 108 +1350 1,458	93 × 26 558 +1860 2,418	78 × 57 546 +3900 4,446
45 × 37 315 +1350 1,665	67 × 88 536 +5360 5,896	72 × 39 648 +2160 2,808	83 × 50 00 +4150 4,150	46 × 74 184 +3220 3,404

Page 69

Name ______________________ Multiplication: 3 Digits × 2 Digits

Multiply. Then add the products.

674 × 27 4718 +13480 18,198	450 × 65 2250 +27000 29,250	917 × 25 4585 +18340 22,925	542 × 73 1626 +37940 39,566	406 × 26 2436 +8120 10,556
853 × 74 3412 +59710 63,122	346 × 54 1384 +17300 18,684	902 × 48 7216 +36080 43,296	300 × 46 1800 +12000 13,800	761 × 25 3805 +15220 19,025
674 × 27 4718 +13480 18,198	808 × 34 3232 +24240 27,472	432 × 59 3888 +21,600 25,488	735 × 74 2940 +51450 54,390	207 × 98 1656 +18630 20,286
327 × 58 2616 +16350 18,966	772 × 48 6176 +30880 37,056	307 × 59 2763 +15350 18,113	912 × 79 8208 +63840 72,048	686 × 68 5488 +41160 46,648

Page 70

Name ______________________ Division, divisors of 1, 2, 3

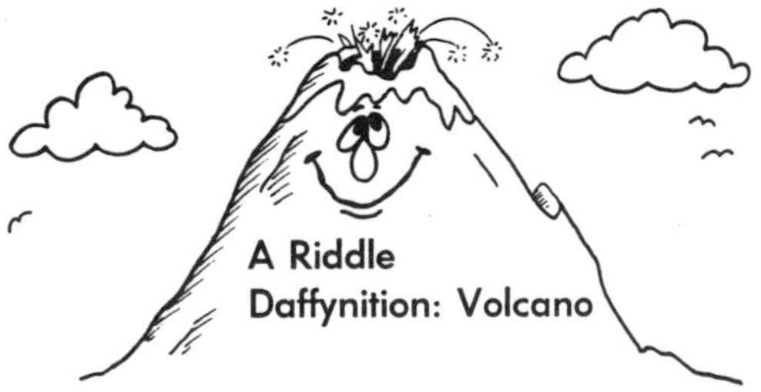

a mountain that (1 7 9 11 3 0 1 10 3 / 0 8 1 0)

blows its top. (2 4 9 5 / 10 0 5 / 0 9 6)

A: 1 ⟌1 = 1	B: 2 ⟌4 = 2	H: 2 ⟌16 = 8	I: 1 ⟌10 = 10
L: 2 ⟌8 = 4	M: 1 ⟌7 = 7	N: 3 ⟌9 = 3	O: 2 ⟌18 = 9
P: 2 ⟌12 = 6	S: 2 ⟌10 = 5	T: 3 ⟌0 = 0	U: 1 ⟌11 = 11

Page 71

Name ______________________ Division, divisors of 1, 2, 3

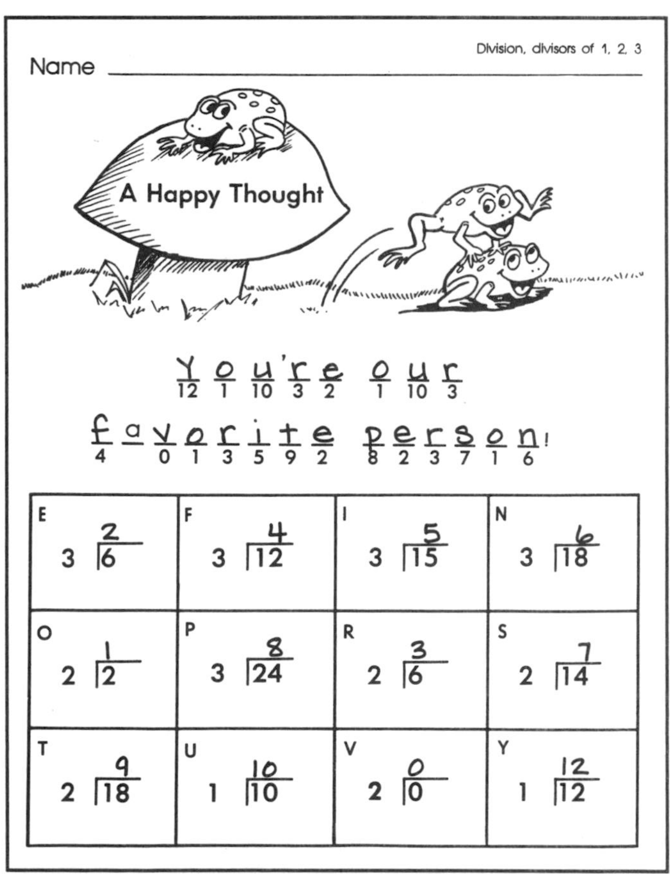

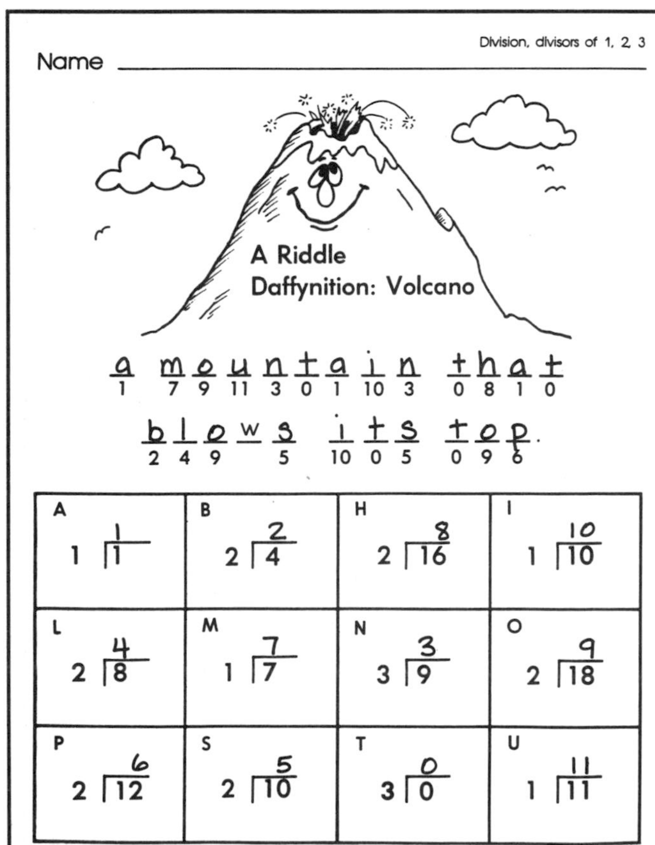

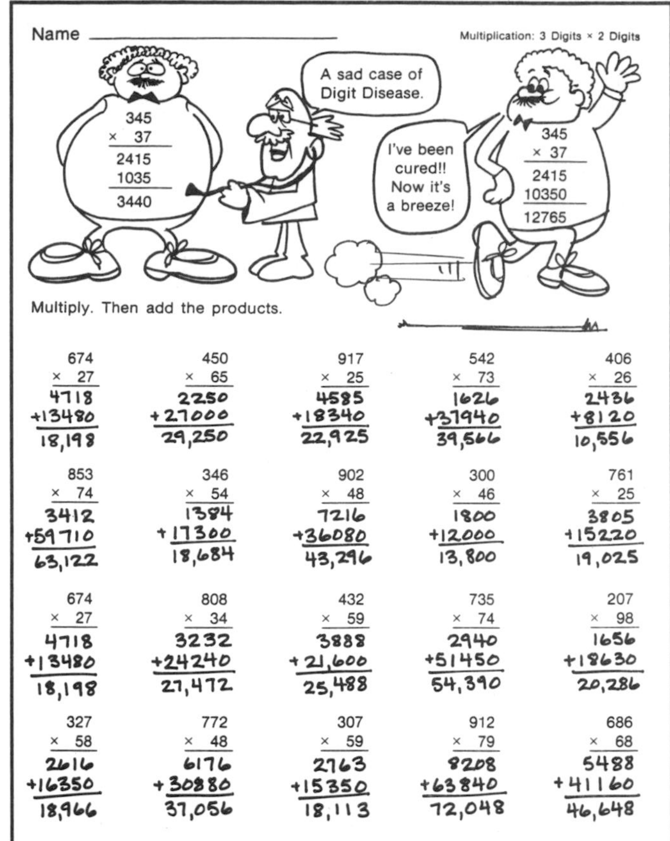

You're our (12 1 10 3 2 / 1 10 3)

favorite person! (4 0 1 3 5 9 2 / 8 2 3 7 1 6)

E: 3 ⟌6 = 2	F: 3 ⟌12 = 4	I: 3 ⟌15 = 5	N: 3 ⟌18 = 6
O: 2 ⟌2 = 1	P: 3 ⟌24 = 8	R: 2 ⟌6 = 3	S: 2 ⟌14 = 7
T: 2 ⟌18 = 9	U: 1 ⟌10 = 10	V: 2 ⟌0 = 0	Y: 1 ⟌12 = 12

Page 72

Answer Key

Name ______________________________ Division, divisors of 1, 2, 3

A Riddle

The answer: a Roadhog
Then what's the question?

what animal has a car?

w	h	a	t		a	n	i	m	a	l		h	a	s		a		c	a	r
10	2	8	1		8	0	9	6	8	4		2	8	3		8		5	8	7

A: $16 \div 2 = 8$	C: $15 \div 3 = 5$	C: $10 \div 2 = 5$	H: $2 \div 1 = 2$
I: $18 \div 2 = 9$	L: $12 \div 3 = 4$	M: $12 \div 2 = 6$	N: $0 \div 1 = 0$
R: $14 \div 2 = 7$	S: $9 \div 3 = 3$	T: $2 \div 2 = 1$	W: $10 \div 1 = 10$

Page 73

Name ______________________________ Division, divisors of 1, 3

A Happy Thought

keep smiling, super kid!

k	e	e	p		s	m	i	l	i	n	g		s	u	p	e	r		k	i	d
3	1	1	9		2	7	8	4	8	5	6		2	12	9	1	0		3	8	10

D: $10 \div 1 = 10$	E: $3 \div 3 = 1$	G: $18 \div 3 = 6$	I: $24 \div 3 = 8$
K: $9 \div 3 = 3$	L: $12 \div 3 = 4$	M: $21 \div 3 = 7$	N: $15 \div 3 = 5$
P: $27 \div 3 = 9$	R: $0 \div 1 = 0$	S: $6 \div 3 = 2$	U: $12 \div 1 = 12$

Page 74

Name ______________________________ Division, divisors of 1, 3, 4

A Tongue Twister

A shy sly spider spied seven seals.

A		s	h	y		s	l	y		s	p	i	d	e	r
8		5	11	1		5	9	1		5	3	2	6	4	7

s	p	i	e	d		s	e	v	e	n		s	e	a	l	s
5	3	2	4	6		5	4	10	4	0		5	4	8	9	5

A: $32 \div 4 = 8$	D: $24 \div 4 = 6$	E: $16 \div 4 = 4$	H: $11 \div 1 = 11$
I: $8 \div 4 = 2$	L: $36 \div 4 = 9$	N: $0 \div 3 = 0$	P: $12 \div 4 = 3$
R: $28 \div 4 = 7$	S: $20 \div 4 = 5$	V: $10 \div 1 = 10$	Y: $4 \div 4 = 1$

Page 75

Name ______________________________ Division, divisors of 1, 4, 5

Wheeeeeeeee!

A Riddle
How do you make an elephant float?

a scoop of chocolate elephant and some root beer

a		s	c	o	o	p		o	f
8			7	2	2	0		2	9

c	h	o	c	o	l	a	t	e		e	l	e	p	h	a	n	t
7	6	2	7	2	3	8	12	4		4	3	4	0	6	8	5	12

and	some	r	o	o	t		b	e	e	r
		10	2	2	12		11	4	4	10

A: $32 \div 4 = 8$	B: $11 \div 1 = 11$	C: $35 \div 5 = 7$	E: $20 \div 5 = 4$
F: $45 \div 5 = 9$	H: $24 \div 4 = 6$	L: $12 \div 4 = 3$	N: $25 \div 5 = 5$
O: $8 \div 4 = 2$	P: $0 \div 5 = 0$	R: $10 \div 1 = 10$	T: $12 \div 1 = 12$

Page 76

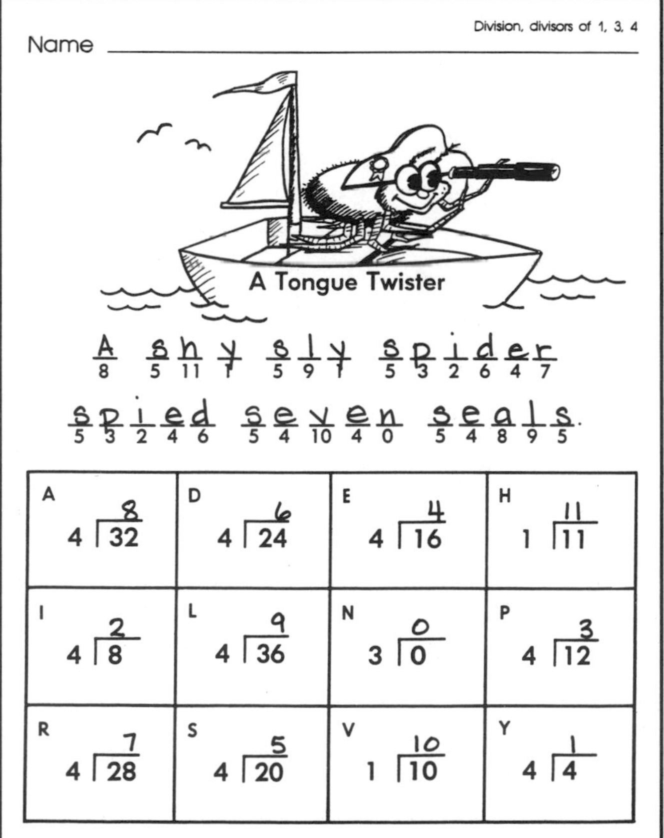

Answer Key

Division, divisors of 5, 6

Name ________________________________

A Happy Thought
Yeah Yeah
Yeah!

I really like you today.

8 | 7 4 1 2 2 0 | 2 8 3 4 | 0 6 10 | 9 6 5 1 0

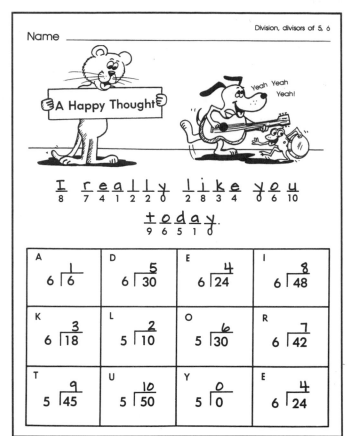

A $6\overline{)6}$ **1**	D $6\overline{)30}$ **5**	E $6\overline{)24}$ **4**	I $6\overline{)48}$ **8**
K $6\overline{)18}$ **3**	L $5\overline{)10}$ **2**	O $5\overline{)30}$ **6**	R $6\overline{)42}$ **7**
T $5\overline{)45}$ **9**	U $5\overline{)50}$ **10**	Y $5\overline{)0}$ **0**	E $6\overline{)24}$ **4**

Page 77

Division, divisors of 5, 6

Name ________________________________

A Riddle
What did the ocean say
when Superman flew over it?

Nothing. It only waved.

3 10 8 1 3 4 | 8 | 10 3 6 9 | 12 5 0 7 2

A $6\overline{)30}$ **5**	D $5\overline{)10}$ **2**	E $6\overline{)42}$ **7**	G $5\overline{)20}$ **4**
H $5\overline{)5}$ **1**	L $6\overline{)36}$ **6**	N $5\overline{)15}$ **3**	O $5\overline{)50}$ **10**
T $6\overline{)48}$ **8**	V $6\overline{)0}$ **0**	W $1\overline{)12}$ **12**	Y $6\overline{)54}$ **9**

Page 78

Division, divisors of 1, 7

Name ________________________________

I beg your pardon!

A Riddle
Riddle: Why are elephants so wrinkled?

Have you ever tried to iron one?

4 1 0 5 | 12 9 8 | 5 0 5 6 | 3 6 10 5 7 | 3 9 | 10 6 9 2 | 9 2 5

A $7\overline{)7}$ **1**	D $7\overline{)49}$ **7**	E $7\overline{)35}$ **5**	H $7\overline{)28}$ **4**
I $1\overline{)10}$ **10**	N $7\overline{)14}$ **2**	O $7\overline{)63}$ **9**	R $7\overline{)42}$ **6**
T $7\overline{)21}$ **3**	U $7\overline{)56}$ **8**	V $7\overline{)0}$ **0**	Y $1\overline{)12}$ **12**

Page 79

Division, divisors of 1, 6, 7

Name ________________________________

A Riddle
What sheet can't
be washed?

a sheet of wrapping paper

3 4 7 7 8 | 0 5 | 11 6 9 9 2 10 1 | 9 9 7 6

E $7\overline{)49}$ **7**	F $7\overline{)35}$ **5**	G $6\overline{)6}$ **1**	H $7\overline{)28}$ **4**
I $6\overline{)12}$ **2**	N $1\overline{)10}$ **10**	O $6\overline{)0}$ **0**	P $7\overline{)63}$ **9**
R $7\overline{)42}$ **6**	S $7\overline{)21}$ **3**	T $7\overline{)56}$ **8**	W $1\overline{)11}$ **11**

Page 80

Answer Key

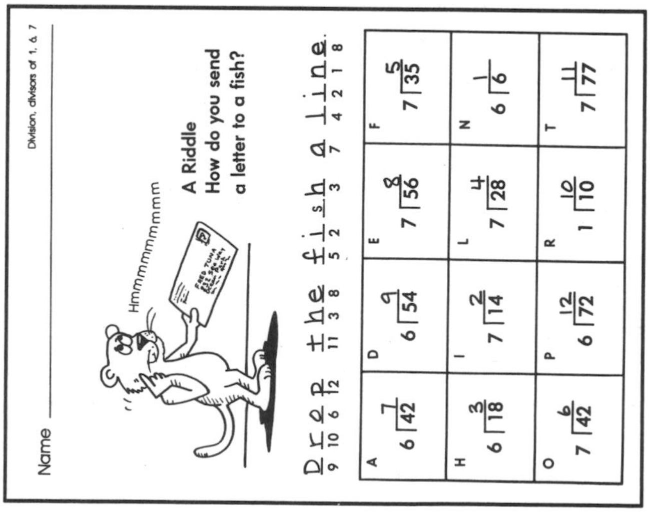

A 6)42 = 7	D 6)54 = 9	E 7)56 = 8	F 7)35 = 5
H 6)18 = 3	I 7)14 = 2	L 7)28 = 4	N 6)6 = 1
O 7)42 = 6	P 6)72 = 12	R 1)10 = 10	T 7)77 = 11

Page 81

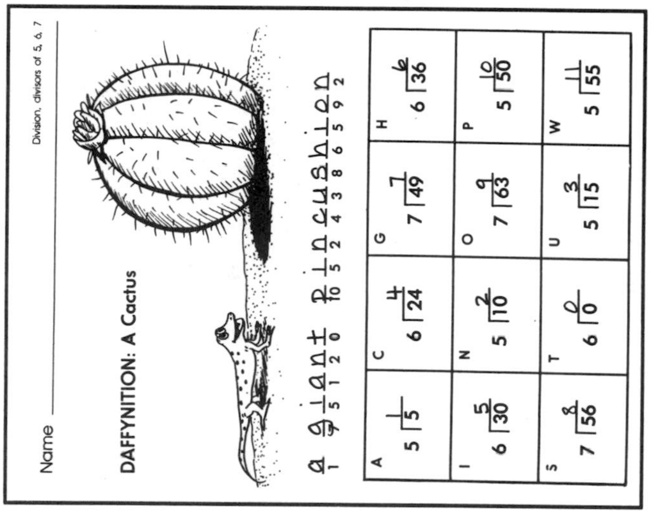

A 5)5 = 1	C 6)24 = 4	G 7)49 = 7	H 6)36 = 6
I 6)30 = 5	N 5)10 = 2	O 7)63 = 9	P 5)50 = 10
S 7)56 = 8	T 6)0 = 0	U 5)15 = 3	W 5)55 = 11

Page 82

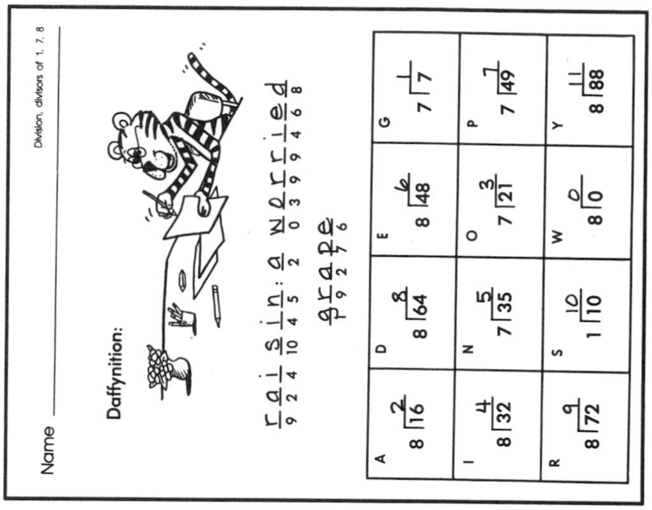

A 8)16 = 2	D 8)64 = 8	E 8)48 = 6	G 7)7 = 1
I 8)32 = 4	N 7)35 = 5	O 7)21 = 3	P 7)49 = 7
R 8)72 = 9	S 1)10 = 10	W 8)0 = 0	Y 8)88 = 11

Page 83

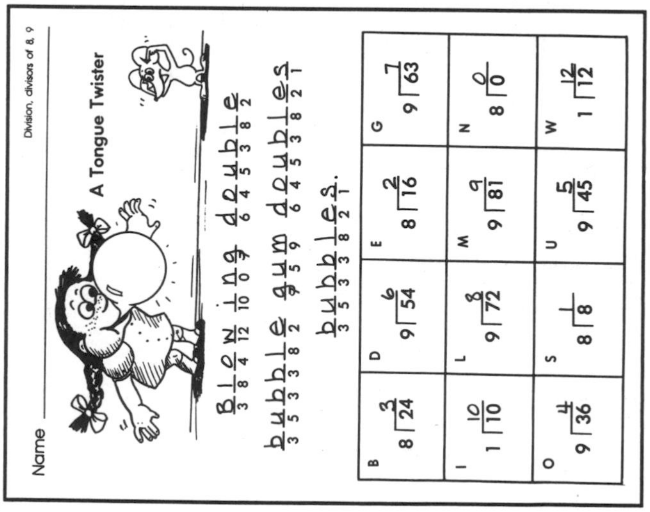

B 8)24 = 3	D 9)54 = 6	E 8)16 = 2	G 9)63 = 7
I 1)10 = 10	L 9)72 = 8	M 9)81 = 9	N 8)0 = 0
O 9)36 = 4	S 8)8 = 1	U 9)45 = 5	W 1)12 = 12

Page 84

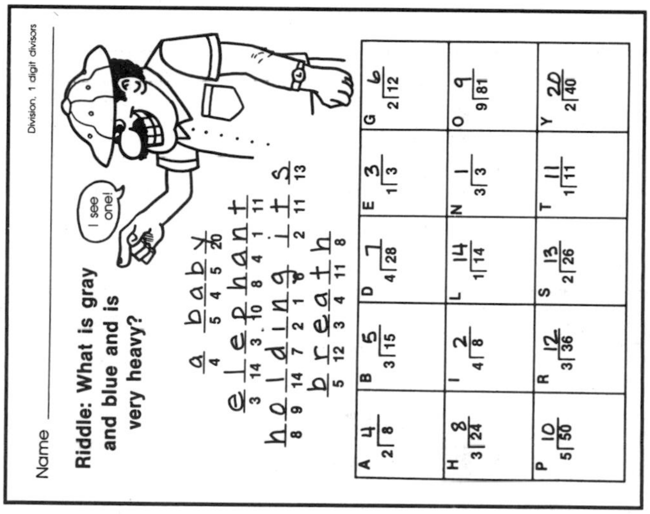

A 2)8 = 4	B 3)15 = 5	D 4)28 = 7	E 1)3 = 3	G 2)12 = 6
H 3)24 = 8	I 4)8 = 2	L 1)14 = 14	N 3)3 = 1	O 9)81 = 9
P 5)50 = 10	R 3)36 = 12	S 2)26 = 13	T 1)11 = 11	Y 2)40 = 20

Page 85

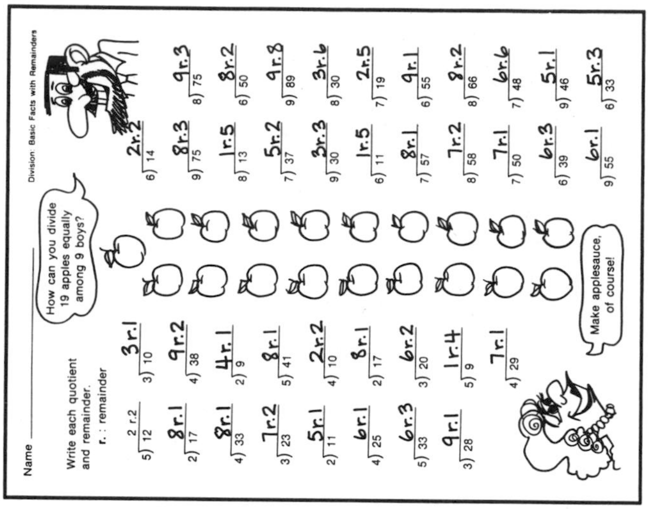

Page 86

Answer Key

Page 89

Page 92

Name

Long Division: 3-Digit Dividend

Divide, Multiply, Subtract, Pull Down — 1. ÷ 2. × 3. - 4. P.D. — Repeat — Divide, Multiply, Subtract — 1. ÷ 2. × 3. -

6) 374 = 62 r. 2 (Examples, Inc.!)

Find the quotients.

4) 304 = 76; 9) 756 = 84; 5) 390 = 78; 7) 196 = 28

3) 201 = 67; 8) 512 = 64; 6) 222 = 37

Find the quotients and remainders.

4) 187 = 46 r. 3; 8) 339 = 42 r. 3; 7) 268 = 38 r. 2; 3) 176 = 58 r. 2

7) 400 = 57 r. 1; 6) 215 = 35 r. 5; 9) 319 = 35 r. 4; 4) 107 = 26 r. 3

Page 88

Page 91

Name

Long Division: 2-Digit Dividend

4 Steps to Success — Divide, Multiply, Subtract, Pull Down — 1. ÷ 2. × 3. - 4. P.D. — Repeat — Divide, Multiply, Subtract — 1. ÷ 2. × 3. -

2) 72 = 36; 8) 96 = 12; 6) 84 = 14; 7) 91 = 13; 3) 87 = 29

2) 74 = 37; 5) 90 = 18; 7) 84 = 12; 6) 96 = 16; 5) 75 = 15

Find the quotients and remainders.

5) 68 = 13 r. 3; 2) 71 = 35 r. 1; 6) 79 = 13 r. 1; 7) 94 = 13 r. 3; 4) 75 = 18 r. 3

3) 74 = 24 r. 2; 6) 94 = 15 r. 4; 3) 47 = 15 r. 2; 7) 99 = 14 r. 1; 6) 88 = 14 r. 4

Page 87

Page 90

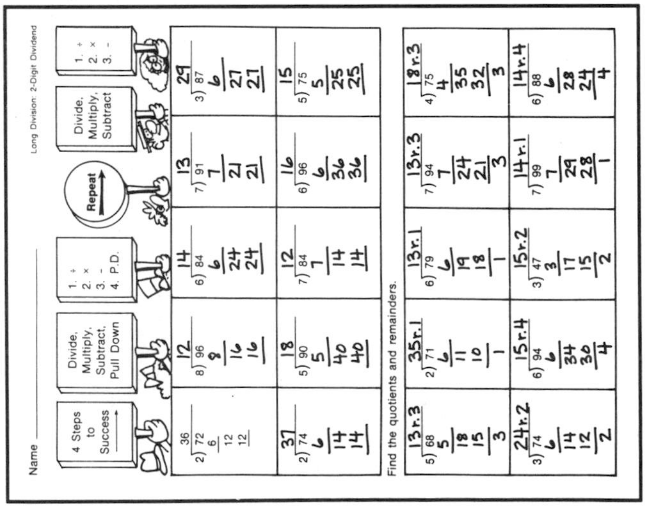

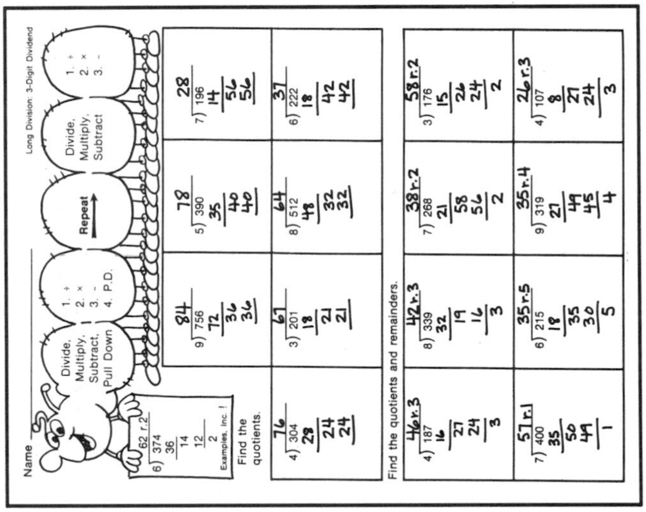

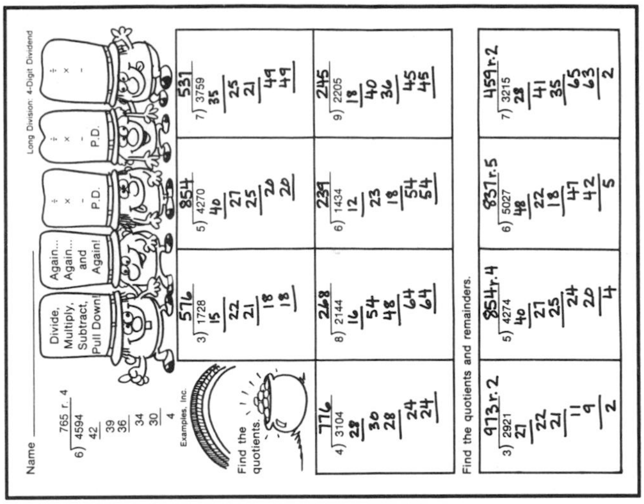

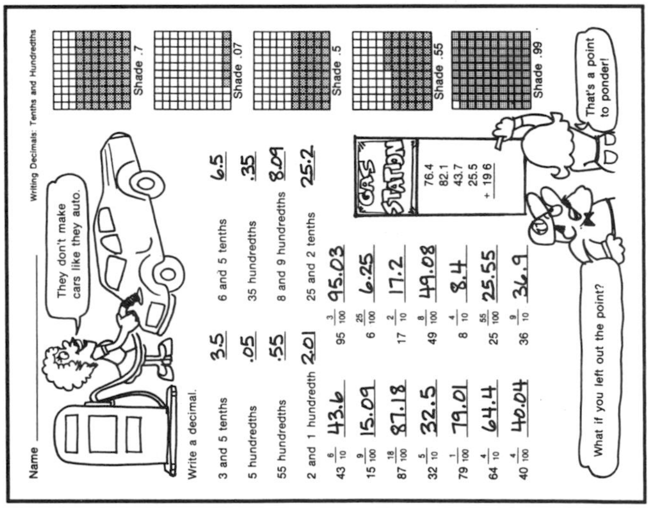

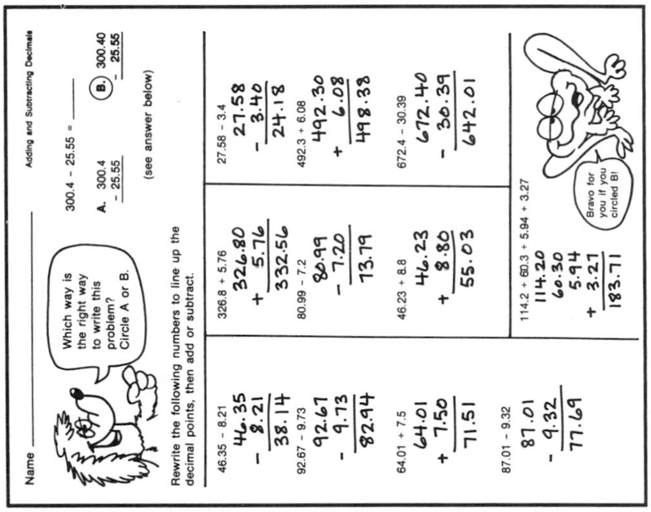

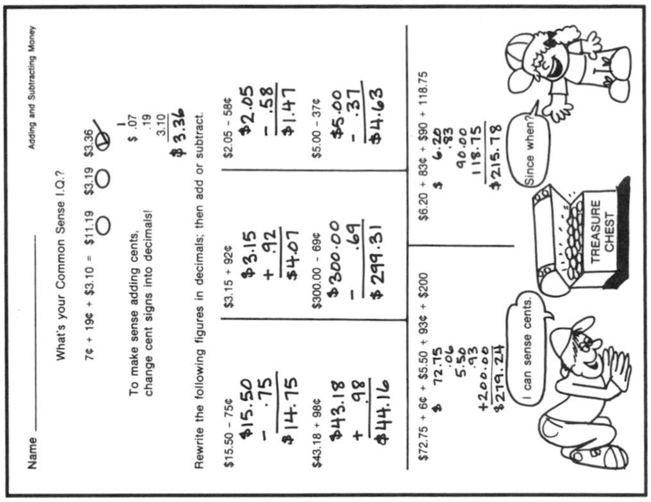

Answer Key

Page 93

Name ____________

CROSS-NUMERAL PUZZLE

					8	3	7					
			1		1		5		1			
	3		2	0	5		4	8	5		4	
3	6	7	8						3	7	5	8
	0		6	5	4		4	5	6		0	
			3		8		3		0			
					2	0	1					

ACROSS
- A. 465 + 372
- F. 824 − 619
- G. 700 − 215
- I. 6,521 − 2,843
- J. 2,774 + 984
- K. 872 − 218
- M. 198 + 258
- N. 37 + 164

DOWN
- A. 939 − 124
- B. 658 + 96
- C. 7,496 + 5,367
- D. 8,064+ 7,296
- E. 57 + 83 + 220
- H. 29 + 68 + 353
- L. 3,000 − 2,518
- M. 219 + 212

Page 94

Name ____________ Skill: Multiplying by 0, 1, 2, 3, and 4

Multiplication Backstroke

Multiply and write the answers. Score ___ 50

A. 2x5 = 10 1x3 = 3 0x9 = 0 1x2 = 2 0x2 = 0
B. 3x4 = 12 2x0 = 0 3x0 = 0 2x3 = 6 1x7 = 7
C. 0x5 = 0 4x4 = 16 3x7 = 21 0x0 = 0 4x5 = 20
D. 4x8 = 32 1x0 = 0 0x6 = 0 2x8 = 16 2x7 = 14
E. 4x2 = 8 1x9 = 9
F. 1x5 = 5 2x1 = 2
G. 1x4 = 4 4x9 = 36 4x1 = 4 2x9 = 18 3x8 = 24
H. 3x6 = 18 3x5 = 15 0x7 = 0 4x0 = 0 0x1 = 0
I. 3x1 = 3 0x3 = 0 4x6 = 24
J. 1x1 = 1 3x9 = 27 1x8 = 8
K. 4x7 = 28 3x3 = 9 2x6 = 12 1x6 = 6 0x8 = 0
L. 2x2 = 4 2x4 = 8 4x3 = 12 0x4 = 0 3x2 = 6

Brainwork! If Kara swims 9 laps four times a week, how many laps does she swim each week? (36 laps)

Page 95

Name ____________ Skill: Multiplying by 5, 6, 7, 8, and 9

Kangaroo Fun

Multiply and write the answers.

A. 3 x 7 = 21, 5 x 9 = 45, 0 x 6 = 0, 4 x 5 = 20, 1 x 8 = 8, 9 x 7 = 63, 3 x 6 = 18, 2 x 8 = 16, 8 x 5 = 40, 4 x 9 = 36

B. 6 x 8 = 48, 8 x 9 = 72, 5 x 6 = 30, 1 x 5 = 5, 4 x 7 = 28, 0 x 9 = 0, 8 x 6 = 48, 3 x 5 = 15, 7 x 7 = 49, 9 x 8 = 72

C. 5 x 5 = 25, 6 x 6 = 36, 2 x 7 = 14, 0 x 8 = 0, 3 x 9 = 27, 7 x 5 = 35, 1 x 9 = 9, 4 x 8 = 32, 9 x 6 = 54, 6 x 7 = 42

D. 7 x 6 = 42, 0 x 5 = 0, 9 x 9 = 81, 1 x 7 = 7, 3 x 8 = 24, 7 x 9 = 63, 2 x 5 = 10, 8 x 7 = 56, 5 x 8 = 40, 2 x 6 = 12

E. 1 x 6 = 6, 7 x 8 = 56, 6 x 5 = 30, 6 x 9 = 54, 5 x 7 = 35, 9 x 5 = 45, 2 x 9 = 18, 4 x 6 = 24, 8 x 8 = 64, 0 x 7 = 0

Score ___ 50

Brainwork! Write a word problem about kangaroos that can be solved using a multiplication fact from this page.

Page 96

Name ____________ Skill: Multiplication facts, 0–9 as factors

Busy Elves

These elves are making multiplication blocks. Solve the problems below. Then find out how many sides each block has by shading in the boxes with odd-numbered answers.

A.	5 x5 = 25	1 x3 = 3	9 x7 = 63	6 x5 = 30	9 x5 = 45	9 x8 = 72	1 x7 = 7	2 x2 = 4	2 x9 = 18	4 x7 = 28	9 x3 = 27
B.	5 x1 = 5	6 x8 = 48	4 x2 = 8	8 x7 = 56	3 x3 = 9	4 x4 = 16	7 x2 = 14	7 x3 = 21	6 x6 = 36	1 x1 = 1	8 x8 = 64
C.	7 x9 = 63	3 x1 = 3	9 x3 = 27	9 x4 = 36	7 x7 = 49	3 x2 = 6	8 x3 = 24	5 x8 = 40	9 x9 = 81	2 x5 = 10	4 x6 = 24
D.	0 x3 = 0	7 x6 = 42	1 x5 = 5	8 x0 = 0	5 x3 = 15	6 x9 = 54	2 x8 = 16	7 x9 = 63	6 x3 = 18	1 x9 = 9	2 x6 = 12
E.	5 x7 = 35	5 x9 = 45	3 x5 = 15	8 x4 = 32	9 x1 = 9	3 x4 = 12	7 x1 = 7	0 x0 = 0	6 x2 = 12	5 x4 = 20	3 x9 = 27

Brainwork! Build your own block out of paper or clay. Write a multiplication fact on each side.

Page 97

Name ____________ Skill: Multiplication facts, 0–9 as factors

Tracking Down Facts

Write the missing factor or product.

A. 6 x 5 = 30, 8 x 4 = 32, 7 x 3 = 21, 9 x 9 = 81, 0 x 4 = 0, 9 x 3 = 27, 6 x 2 = 12, 4 x 4 = 16, 8 x 5 = 40, 3 x 3 = 9

B. 3 x 8 = 24, 5 x 4 = 20, 0 x 3 = 0, 8 x 1 = 8, 2 x 7 = 14, 5 x 5 = 25, 6 x 9 = 54, 6 x 4 = 24, 7 x 6 = 42, 3 x 4 = 12

C. 2 x 5 = 10, 7 x 7 = 49, 3 x 5 = 15, 8 x 2 = 16, 6 x 6 = 36, 9 x 7 = 63, 5 x 9 = 45, 2 x 2 = 4, 1 x 0 = 0, 3 x 6 = 18

D. 2 x 4 = 8, 1 x 7 = 7, 6 x 8 = 48, 8 x 5 = 40, 3 x 1 = 3, 5 x 7 = 35, 8 x 9 = 72, 3 x 2 = 6, 7 x 4 = 28, 8 x 8 = 64

E. 9 x 4 = 36, 5 x 6 = 30, 1 x 7 = 7, 1 x 5 = 5, 0 x 6 = 0, 1 x 1 = 1, 4 x 9 = 36, 2 x 9 = 18, 0 x 2 = 0, 7 x 8 = 56

Score ___ 50

Brainwork! Write four multiplication problems that have 7 as a missing factor.

Page 98

Name ____________ Skill: Multiplication facts, 0–9 as factors

Football Fun

SCOREBOARD ___ / 100

Solve by multiplying.

A.	8 x5 = 40	5 x3 = 15	6 x1 = 6	0 x0 = 0	4 x9 = 36	1 x2 = 2	3 x7 = 21	9 x2 = 18	8 x9 = 72	2 x9 = 18
B.	9 x1 = 9	1 x3 = 3	2 x6 = 12	0 x9 = 0	3 x3 = 9	6 x9 = 54	4 x6 = 24	9 x6 = 54	7 x0 = 0	3 x5 = 15
C.	6 x3 = 18	0 x3 = 0	5 x1 = 5	4 x1 = 4	9 x0 = 0	6 x2 = 12	2 x7 = 14	5 x2 = 10	1 x4 = 4	7 x6 = 42
D.	7 x8 = 56	2 x3 = 6	7 x1 = 7	1 x5 = 5	4 x4 = 16	0 x1 = 0	5 x4 = 20	9 x7 = 63	8 x7 = 56	3 x9 = 27
E.	8 x1 = 8	1 x1 = 1	6 x6 = 36	5 x9 = 45	3 x0 = 0	6 x7 = 42	4 x7 = 28	3 x8 = 24	6 x0 = 0	9 x5 = 45
F.	0 x8 = 0	4 x3 = 12	2 x2 = 4	8 x0 = 0	2 x8 = 16	4 x2 = 8	1 x7 = 7	7 x2 = 14	5 x0 = 0	7 x3 = 21
G.	1 x8 = 8	6 x4 = 24	3 x1 = 3	2 x0 = 0	8 x8 = 64	0 x4 = 0	5 x5 = 25	3 x2 = 6	9 x4 = 36	7 x5 = 35
H.	8 x3 = 24	1 x6 = 6	0 x6 = 0	5 x6 = 30	3 x4 = 12	2 x4 = 8	7 x7 = 49	8 x6 = 48	6 x5 = 30	0 x5 = 0
I.	6 x8 = 48	9 x3 = 27	2 x1 = 2	4 x0 = 0	4 x8 = 32	0 x2 = 0	5 x7 = 35	9 x2 = 18	1 x0 = 0	7 x9 = 63
J.	5 x8 = 40	3 x6 = 18	2 x5 = 10	7 x4 = 28	4 x5 = 20	8 x2 = 16	0 x7 = 0	9 x6 = 54	8 x4 = 32	1 x9 = 9

Brainwork! Write a football word problem that uses one of these multiplication facts.

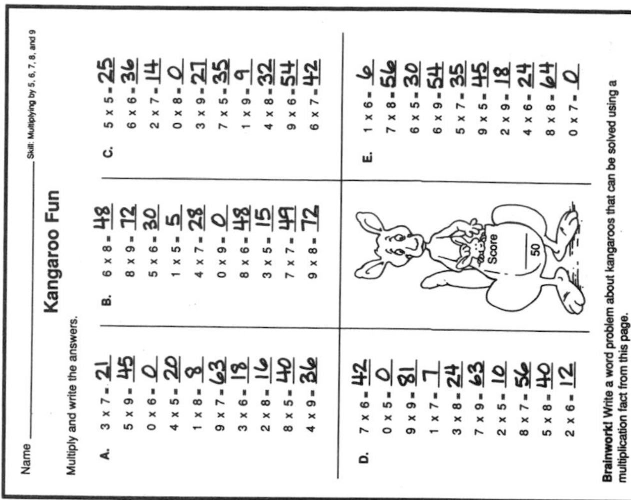

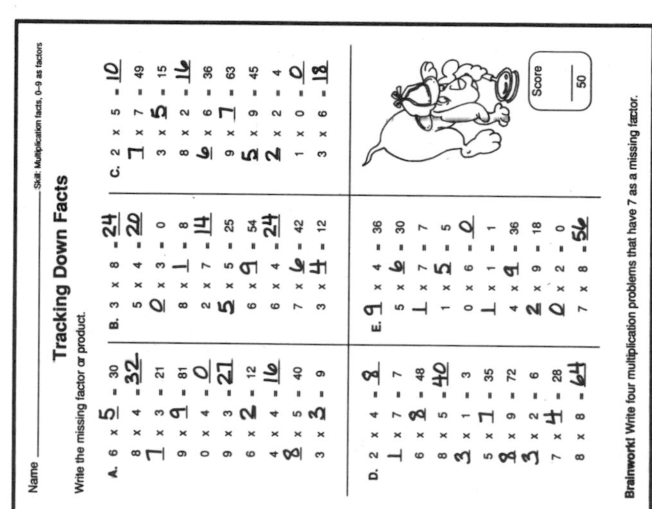

Answer Key

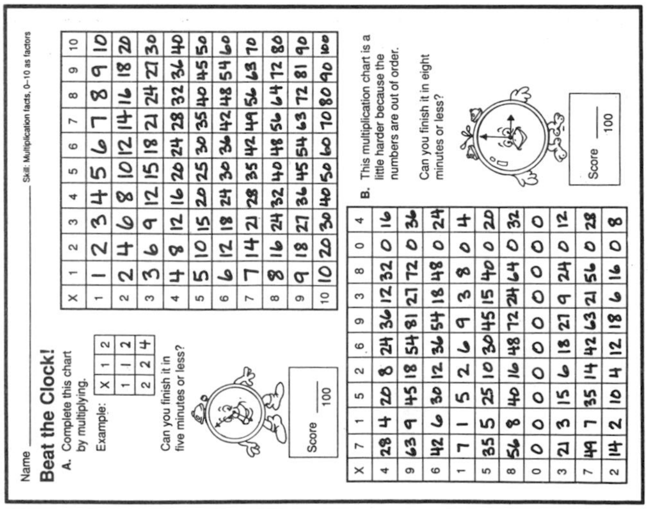

Page 99

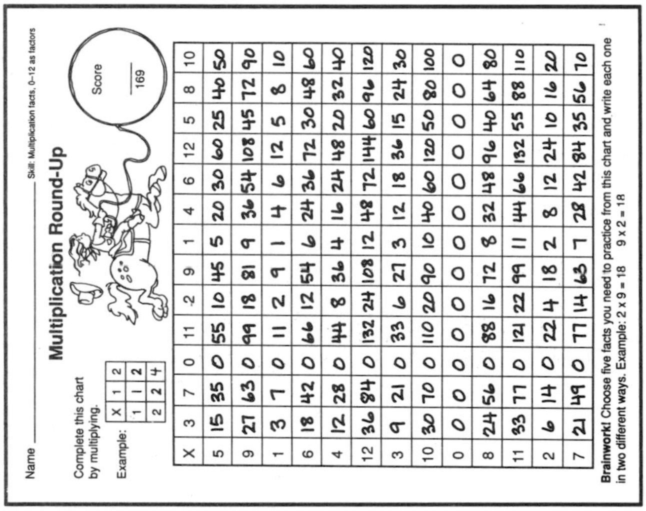

Page 100

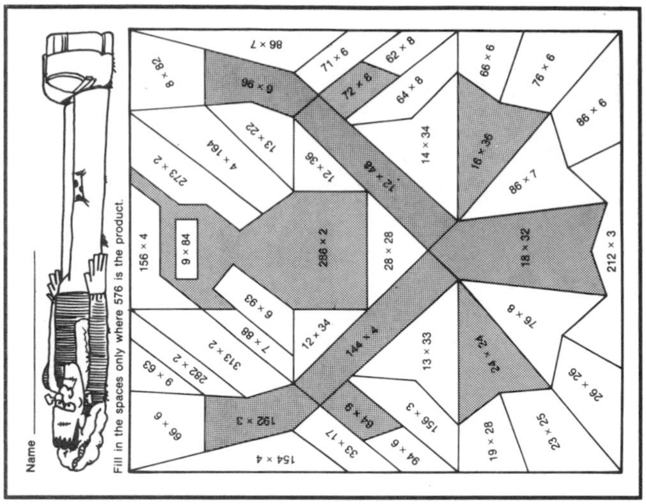

Page 101

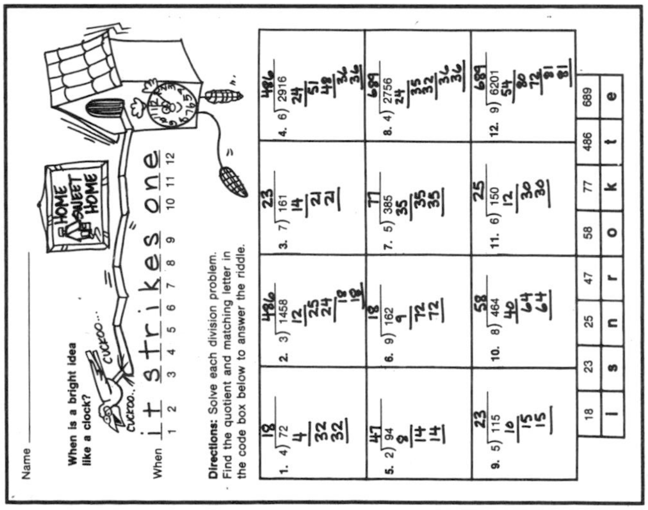

Page 102

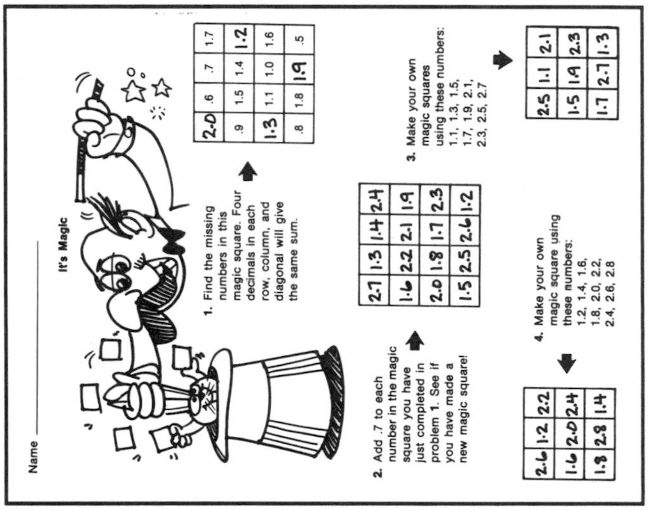

Page 103

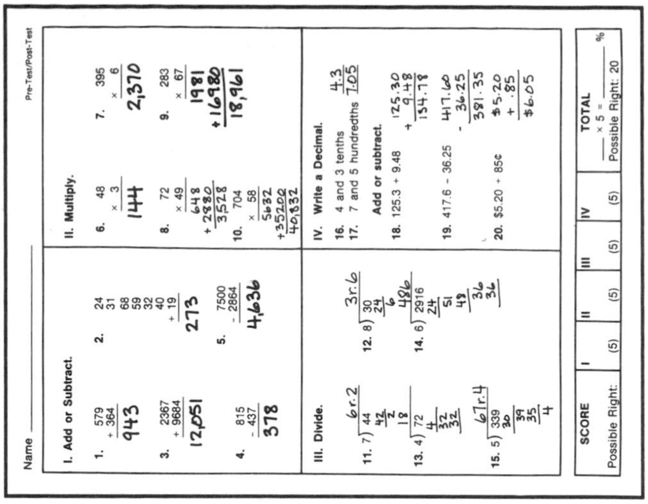

Page 104